THE CIVIL WAR
IN
LOUDOUN COUNTY

VIRGINIA

THE CIVIL WAR
IN
LOUDOUN COUNTY

VIRGINIA

A HISTORY OF HARD TIMES

STEVAN F. MESERVE

WITH A CHAPTER ON BALL'S BLUFF BY JAMES A. MORGAN III

Charleston · London

THE
History
PRESS

Published by The History Press
Charleston, SC 29403
www.historypress.net

Cover design by Marshall Hudson.

First published 2008
Second printing 2008
Third printing 2009
Fourth printing 2011
Fifth printing 2011

Manufactured in the United States

ISBN 978.1.59629.378.6

Library of Congress Cataloging-in-Publication Data

Meserve, Stevan F.
The Civil War in Loudoun County, Virginia : a history of hard times /
Stevan F. Meserve.
p. cm.
Includes bibliographical references and index.
ISBN-13: 978-1-59629-378-6 (alk. paper)
1. Loudoun County (Va.)--History, Military--19th century. 2. Loudoun
County (Va.)--History--19th century. 3. Loudoun County (Va.)--Social
conditions--19th century. 4. Virginia--History--Civil War,
1861-1865--Campaigns. 5. Virginia--History--Civil War, 1861-1865--Social
aspects. 6. United States--History--Civil War, 1861-1865--Campaigns. 7.
United States--History--Civil War, 1861-1865--Social aspects. I. Title.
F232.L8M47 2008
973.7'30975528--dc22
2007047744

Contents

Acknowledgements

The hardest thing about writing this book has been deciding what to leave out to avoid bogging the reader down in more detail than an overview like this allows. It is not nearly as difficult to know whom to thank for assistance and inspiration, without which the book would not have been written.

As unoriginal as it may be, I have to start by thanking my wife, who has endured my passion for Civil War history and research for more years than she cares to admit. She and I have come to an understanding. I can traipse across battlefields or huddle in musty archives all I want as long as I don't demand that she come along. I do have to remember to invite her, however, when a research trip or battlefield tour involves visiting an old home.

Special thanks are in order for my longtime research associate, Rebecca Fitzgerald, and her husband, Ed. Losing them to the Lynchburg area was like losing an arm. I would be in despair if we could not still collaborate on our research projects via e-mail. Likewise, I would be lost without the help and encouragement of Anne Hughes, a skilled researcher whose home is in Robin Hood country in the United Kingdom, and Tonia "Teej" Smith of North Carolina, the best editor with whom I have ever been privileged to work.

Words are inadequate to express my appreciation to James A. Morgan III, who wrote the chapter on the Battle of Ball's Bluff. Jim is not only an authority who has spent years researching the subject and who has written his own book on the battle, but he is also one of the founders of an outstanding corps of battlefield guides. The quality of this work is greatly enhanced by maps drawn by David Woodbury, who has also encouraged me for years to put some of this information on paper.

Like everyone who has researched Loudoun County history in recent years, I am indebted to Mary Fishback and the staff of the Thomas Balch Library, and to Wynne Saffer—all of whom have patiently answered my questions, endured my foolishness and pointed me in the right direction to find the information I needed. Similar appreciation is in order for the staff of the National Archives in Washington and for Sue Collins of the Jefferson County Museum in Charles Town, West Virginia, a repository of the most complete record of Colonel R. Preston Chew, a Loudoun boy who made good in the horse artillery. For the Quaker community papers and letters quoted in this work, I am indebted to Bronwen Souders and the Waterford Foundation.

I owe a great debt of gratitude to my friend and mentor John Divine, "The Sage of Loudoun County," whose encyclopedic knowledge of Loudoun history has inspired every would-be historian fortunate enough to have known him. The list of departed friends who helped me over the years of my research into Loudoun history lies heavy on my heart today: Brian Pohanka, Jim Moyer, Lee Wallace, Ernest "Pete" Peterkin and Virgil Carrington "Pat" Jones are but a few of them. Fortunately, some are still around to hear my thanks for their help and encouragement: Don Hakenson, Gregg Dudding, Larry and Keith Rogers, Rob Hodge and Tom Evans. I owe all of them a debt I fear I can never repay.

Introduction

The truth of it is, I think, that the whole country, South included, is just beginning to see the Civil War whole and entire for the first time. The thing was too big and too bloody, too full of suffering and hatred, too closely knit into the fabric of our meaning as a people, to be held off and looked at—until now (1957). It is like a man walking away from a mountain. The bigger it is, the farther he's got to go before he can see it. Then one day he looks back and there it is, this colossal thing lying across his past.[1]

—*Walker Percy*

On May 2, 1861, not long after the voters of Virginia ratified the state's ordinance of secession, Rachel Steer, a young Quaker girl living in Waterford, wrote in her diary, "The prospect of dreadful times coming fills all hearts with gloom."[2] Four long years of warfare, privation and suffering in Loudoun County would bear testimony to her prescience. The generations of people who experienced the American Civil War and knew firsthand the evils of slavery have long since passed away, but many a houseless chimney, fire-blackened bridge abutment and ruined mill in Loudoun County still stand as mute witnesses to the physical cost of the conflict.

In the century and a half since the war ended, its popular image has undergone a drastic transformation from the "Lost Cause" romanticism of the late nineteenth and early twentieth centuries to a modern demonization of all things Confederate. Along the way, the country celebrated the Civil War Centennial in the 1960s with national fanfare, special stamp issues, commemorative trinkets and records and the birth of Civil War reenacting. With thousands of books in print and a number of recent high-budget movies on the subject, the war has not yet faded from memory. Still, each passing year sees more and more historic sites either destroyed or threatened by rampant development. This problem is acute in Loudoun County—one of the fastest-growing jurisdictions in the country. East of Goose Creek, little remains of the wartime terrain, while more historic sites are threatened along the Route 7 (Leesburg Pike) and Route 50 (Little River Turnpike) corridors.

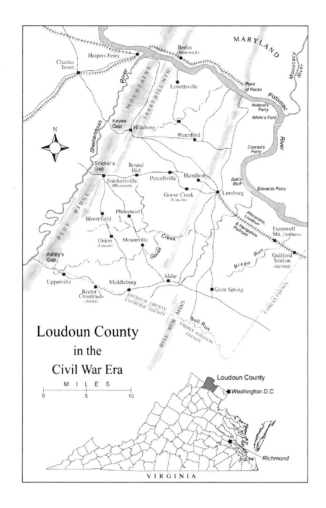

Map drawn by David Woodbury.

The best way to preserve historic sites is to keep an awareness of their significance alive. This book is not an exhaustive history of the war in Loudoun; rather, it is an overview designed to spark an interest in the minds of people who may not know that they walk daily on ground made sacred by the blood of the patriots who wore the blue and gray. Perhaps it will also inspire the old-time families in the county to break out letters and diaries hidden away in attics or basement storerooms to get a firsthand glimpse at what their own ancestors experienced during the war and to share their words with others.

Loudoun may not have seen battles on the scale of Gettysburg or Manassas, but it was a rare day between 1861 and 1865 when the county's residents did not hear shots fired in anger. Rarer still was an opportunity to go to bed with a full stomach and a heart not weighed down with concern for loved ones in the army or family in enemy-occupied territory. The soldiers may have been the only ones who campaigned and died in battle, but everyone suffered and sacrificed. This book is for all of them.

The English Come to Loudoun

The first Englishmen came to Loudoun County late in the seventeenth century, scouting toward the Blue Ridge Mountains for hostile Native American activity. The 1692 journal of a militiaman named David Strahan reveals that he and a small armed party of "Rangers of the Potomack" travelled as far west as the "sugar lands" (the ford across Sugarland Run on the present-day border between Loudoun and Fairfax counties) to monitor "Indian" activity. Then, in 1699, a party sent by the governor of Virginia passed through the area on their way to meet with a Native American band at Conoy Island near the present-day community of Point of Rocks, Maryland. Though none of these men remained in the area long, they brought back glowing descriptions of the land, its abundant wildlife and its sugar maples.

The future Loudoun County was part of the five-million-acre Northern Neck Proprietary that the English king had taken from the Virginia Company in 1624. In September 1649 King Charles I, who was still in exile in France, granted the Northern Neck to seven English noblemen who were among his staunchest supporters: Sir Ralph, Lord Hopton of Stratton (1596–1652); Henry, Lord Jermyn, later Earl of St. Albans (circa 1604–1684); John, Lord Culpeper, First Baron of Thoresway (1600–1660); Sir John, Baron of Berkeley of Stratton (1606–1678); Sir William Morton of Gloucestershire (died 1672); Sir Dudley Wyatt (died 1651); and Lieutenant Colonel Thomas Culpeper (circa 1602–circa 1652). By 1681, Thomas, Second Lord Culpeper, owned most of the shares of the original grant. When he died in 1689, the property went to his daughter, who married Thomas, Fifth Lord Fairfax. It was later inherited by their son, Thomas, Sixth Lord Fairfax.[3]

For thousands of years, people had mostly passed through the area on the way to somewhere else: the Iroquois native tribes moving along a well-established trail that would one day be known as the Carolina Road as they travelled from their summer homes in New York and Pennsylvania to their winter hunting ground in the Carolinas and Georgia, and the English patrolling the area as an early warning against attack on frontier settlements farther east. That changed between 1725 and 1735 when Quaker, German, Irish and Scots-Irish settlers moved down from Pennsylvania into the rich farmlands of the Catoctin Valley. Around that same time, English Cavaliers began to move west from the Piedmont to settle the Loudoun Valley and the area of Sugarland Run.

The Cavaliers brought their slaves with them, settling on large plantations purchased from Robert "King" Carter, the agent for Lord Fairfax, in the eastern and southern portions of the county. The Pennsylvania settlers, on the other hand, established small farms that they worked themselves. With religious strictures against owning or even employing slaves, they established a philosophical division from the other settlers in the area that would define the region all the way through the Civil War.

When the settlers first arrived, Loudoun was still part of Prince William County, which was divided in 1742 into two counties, with the new one named for Lord Fairfax, its proprietor. In 1757, Fairfax County was, in turn, split, with its western portion being named for John Campbell, the Fourth Earl of Loudoun.

The first clerk of the Loudoun County Court was Charles Binns, who held the post from 1757 to 1796. He kept his office in Rokeby and his home south of a small settlement called George Town at the intersection of the Carolina and Old Ridge Roads (now Routes 15 and 7, respectively). Binns was succeeded in office by his son, Charles Binns Jr., who served from 1796 until 1837. As prominent as the Binns family was in the early history of the county, one member would play a dark role in the coming Civil War.

Captain Nicholas Minor of the Virginia militia owned the land around the highway intersection. In 1757, he hired John Hough to survey the property for a town site, laying out half-acre lots. The next year, by order of the county court, lots twenty-seven and twenty-eight were set aside for the construction of a proper courthouse, and the town of Leesburg was "erected" by an act of the Virginia Assembly. Since 1761, when the original building was finished and the lots were formally deeded to the county by Captain Minor, the Loudoun County Courthouse, in its various incarnations, has occupied the same site.

The county grew steadily, but not rapidly, since so much of the land was tied up in large estates. The early settlers, according to James Head,

> *had no costly tastes to gratify, no expensive habits to indulge and neither possessed nor cared for luxuries. Their subsistence, such as they required, cost but little of either time or labor. The corn from which they made their bread came forth from the prolific soil almost at the touch of their rude plows. Their cattle and hogs found abundant sustenance in the broad pastures which, in the summer, yielded the richest grass, and in the woods where, in the fall, the ground was strewn with acorns and other like provender.[4]*

Farming may have been good in the new county, but life was not easy for its people. In 1757, Loudoun was still on the frontier, and the danger of French and Native American attacks on isolated farms and small settlements was very real. The independence of the early settlers and their determination to resist all threats to their new way of life would lead the county to contribute both men and financial support to the Revolution and make it a key player in the establishment of a new country. That same spirit would be manifest in the sons and grandsons of the Revolutionary heroes when they answered the call to defend Virginia against an even greater threat than the English king in 1860.

Slavery and Abolition in Loudoun County

By the time it marked its hundredth anniversary, Loudoun had grown to be one of the most populous counties in the commonwealth. The 1860 census would show it to have 21,774 inhabitants, 15,021 of whom were white, with 1,252 free blacks and 5,501 slaves. The majority of the slaves were held in the southern end of the county along the Ashby's Gap Turnpike (modern Route 50). In 1850, the largest slaveholders in the county were Elizabeth Carter (widow of George Carter) of Oatlands and Bellefield, with 85 slaves; Lewis Berkeley of Aldie, 58; John Peyton Dulany of Welbourne, 52; George Grayson of Newstead, 35; John Armistead Carter of Crednal, 32; Townsend McVeigh of Valley View, 31; and Humphrey Brooke Powell of The Shades, 27. All lived in the Aldie-to-Upperville corridor.[5]

Half of the slave owners in Loudoun County owned fewer than five slaves. Only 2 percent owned twenty or more, and 521 of the 735 farm owners in the county owned no slaves at all. It is a small wonder, then, that Loudoun County was home to several active abolition societies in the 1820s and early 1830s. "As late as 1827," wrote Thomas Earl, "a Virginia convention for the abolition of slavery was held in Loudoun County and seven such local societies were reported."[6] Much of the abolition sentiment was fueled by the religious beliefs of the county's Quaker and German population, but not all. Slavery had been a hotly debated topic since the days of the Continental Congresses, and more than a few of the founding fathers, even those who were slave owners themselves, longed for its end in America.

In the mistaken belief that white men and free blacks could not live peacefully together, many early abolitionists favored shipping freed slaves back to Africa. They established what were known as "colonization societies" to raise money to purchase land in Liberia and pay the cost of transporting freed slaves to new homes there. The largest of these groups, the American Colonization Society,

had thirty-five branches in Virginia in 1832 and included among its supporters all the great names of that day: Monroe, Madison, Marshall, G.W.P. Custis. In 1825 $500 was appropriated for colonization by the [Virginia] Legislature and this subject had been discussed by that body as early as 1800.[7]

Oatlands Plantation, the home of George Carter. *Photo by the author.*

Two factors combined in 1832, however, to diminish and virtually destroy the abolition movement in Virginia. The first was a slave revolt led by Nat Turner of Southampton County, Virginia, in August 1831. Although the uprising lasted less than forty-eight hours, fifty-seven white men, women and children were dead by the time the militia destroyed Turner's small band of followers. Turner himself was captured, tried and executed in November; but the fear of similar uprisings led to the enactment of repressive laws across the state that severely curtailed the rights of all blacks, both slave and free. An official policy was established in which any public criticism of the "peculiar institution" of slavery was forbidden on the grounds that it might encourage future slave revolts.

The second factor working against any sort of moderation in the abolition debate was the increasing stridency of a Boston newspaper publisher named William Lloyd Garrison. Although his fiercely abolitionist newspaper, *The Liberator*, never had a paid subscription list of more than a few hundred people, copies of the paper were widely circulated throughout the country and were believed by many Southerners to reflect the feelings of the entire population of the Northern states. Garrison was a self-confessed extremist who loudly condemned the evil of slavery and the "evil men" who practiced it. In his estimation, Nat Turner's revolt was a sign that the South was finally beginning to reap what it had sown.

No one likes to be told that their society and deeds are evil, and Southerners were no exception. The more virulent the criticism and condemnation heaped upon them by men like Garrison, the more defensive they became of the practice of slavery. Many of the five hundred Loudoun farmers and merchants who owned no slaves rose to defend the practice as an essential part of the Southern economy, and to decry "foreigners" who attacked Virginians without ever having visited the state.

Garrison's repeated calls for *immediate emancipation* pushed the voices of moderate men into the background and the country became increasingly polarized on the slavery question. In 1857, Quaker surveyor Yardley Taylor, the president of the Loudoun Manumission and Emigration Society, was arrested and charged with stealing slaves and spiriting them across the Potomac to freedom in the North. Despite being labeled "the Chief of the abolition clan in Loudoun," Taylor was acquitted for lack of evidence.[8] Whether he was guilty or not, the Underground Railroad definitely ran through Loudoun County in the 1850s. The heavily timbered Blue Ridge Mountains offered abundant hiding places for bands of escaping slaves, while Quakers and others stood ready to help out with food, medical attention and directions to the nearest of several useable fords across the river. At times, their assistance took the form of obstructing slave catchers in their search for fugitives. George Carter of Oatlands wrote bitterly of

> *struggling with the most enthusiastic and invincible opposition in the recovery of my property, from the Quakers and other…[and enduring] the sneers, the contempt, and scorn of the whole mass of aiders, advisors, and accomplices of runaway slaves, who are now triumphing at my shame.*[9]

As the two sides in the abolition debate grew further apart with each passing year, the country witnessed a civil war in the Kansas Territory, where pro- and antislavery men fought a short but bloody conflict to determine whether the new state would enter the Union slave or free. As upsetting to the political debate between North and South as the shots in Kansas might have been, they were nothing compared to those fired literally "next door" to Loudoun County at Harpers Ferry on October 16, 1859. Before dawn that Sunday morning, John Brown, a veteran of the Kansas border war, led eighteen men into town to capture the Federal arsenal there. His plan was to seize nearly a hundred thousand muskets and rifles that were stored in the Federal arsenal and use them to arm the slaves whom he was sure would flee their plantation homes and rally to his call. Moving southward along the line of the Blue Ridge, he planned to bring the economy of Virginia to its knees as its primary labor force abandoned fields and factories for freedom.

Initially, the raid went according to plan. The arsenal, guarded by a single night watchman, was taken easily, as were several hostages gathered from the town and surrounding area. The trouble started when local slaves did not rise up in rebellion against their masters as Brown had hoped. Then, when a railroad baggage handler, a free black man named Heyward Shepherd, tried to warn an eastbound train, Brown's men shot and killed him. The train passed on through the town and quickly spread the alarm all the way to Washington, D.C. Long before the authorities there could respond, local militia companies from Maryland and Virginia began to surround the town, firing at Brown's men from the heights nearby. By noon, all escape routes were in their hands, and Brown and his surviving men and prisoners barricaded themselves inside a brick firehouse. The rest of that day and all through the next, the militia traded shots with the heavily armed raiders, each side losing men in the exchange of fire. By the morning of October 18, a company of Marines under the command of Colonel Robert E. Lee arrived from Washington. Aided by Lieutenant J.E.B. Stuart, who had known Brown in Kansas, they stormed the firehouse, freed the hostages and captured Brown and seven of his men. Although none of the Marines was killed, Brown's men had killed five and wounded nine of the locals. Ten of his own men, including two of his sons, were dead and seven, in addition to him, were taken as prisoners. Five managed to escape.

Brown was taken to Charles Town, the county seat of Jefferson County, and put on trial for the murder of four whites and a black man, inciting slave revolt and treason against Virginia. It took a week of trial and only forty-five minutes of jury deliberation to find him guilty on all three charges. He was sentenced to be hanged on December 2. Brown spent the next month writing letters to supporters and acquaintances in the North. When the letters were published in the newspapers, they gained him a great deal of sympathy, and even such noted men as Victor Hugo wrote to the president to try to secure a pardon and release for him. Every letter, however, enraged the majority of Southerners and convinced them that Northern abolitionists were all ready to incite slave revolt and encourage the slaughter of innocent women and children to secure their ends.

The most lasting effect of John Brown's Raid was a reorganization and modernization of the Virginia Militia system. In effect, John Brown gave Virginia an eighteen-month head start on creating the citizen army it would put into the field in the summer of 1861. In Loudoun County, several new militia companies began recruiting and training soldiers for the defense of the state. By the first week in December, no fewer than three new militia companies were organizing in the county: the Volunteer Corps, which began recruiting on November 4; the Loudoun Guards, which was organized a week later; and the Civic Guard, which came into existence the first week of December. Of the latter, the local newspaper said:

> *The company is composed of some of the best and most respected citizens of the community, many of whose heads are frosted with the snows of more than three score years, but whose breasts are fired with the same zeal that animated our patriot fathers, and who, should the unfortunate occasion ever arise making it necessary, would strike a telling blow in defense of their homes and their family altars…Woe be to the hapless disciple of John Brown whom "being instigated of the devil, and not having the fear of God before his eyes," falls into* [their] *hands.*[10]

Between the ranting of William Lloyd Garrison, who was later revealed to have been one of the "Secret Six" prominent Bostonians financing and arming John Brown and his men, and the raid on Harpers Ferry, renewed fears of slave revolt and new fears of additional armed attacks by Northern abolitionists made more Loudoun County citizens than ever before receptive to the talk of secession coming daily from the states of the Deep South. For the time being, the county remained true to its Whig roots and was predominantly unionist in sentiment—but that would soon change.

Politics and Secession

Seven of the first twelve presidents of the United States (from George Washington to Zachary Taylor) were born in Virginia, and the citizens of the state took great pride in its nickname, "the Mother of Presidents." Virginians felt like they had done more in 1776 to create the country and ensure its survival than all of the other states combined. The commander of the Continental army was a Virginian; the Declaration of Independence was written by a Virginian; and the final, decisive victory of the Revolution was won on Virginia soil at Yorktown. Loyalty to the Union was as natural to Virginians as pride in one's own creation. By 1860, as talk of splitting the country dominated the national news, the political leaders of the state preached moderation and reason. Governor John Letcher called for a convention of all the states to meet to resolve the differences between the North and the slaveholding Southern states.

"If such a Convention shall assemble," he said,

> and after a free and full consultation and comparison of opinions they shall find that the differences between the slaveholding and non-slaveholding States are irreconcilable, let them consider the question of a peaceable separation and the adjustment of all questions relating to the disposition of the common property between the two sections.[11]

Unfortunately, the passions of the country had already been aroused to such a fever pitch that few men wanted to hear talk of compromise and reason. Between the abolitionists of New England and the Fire Eaters of the Deep South lay an emotional gulf too wide to be bridged by rational debate. In the presidential election of 1860, the Republican Party nominated Abraham Lincoln and Hannibal Hamlin, while the Democratic Party split along sectional lines, with the Northern party nominating Stephen A. Douglas and Herschel Johnson while the Southern Democratic Party nominated John C. Breckinridge and Joseph Lane. At the same time, old-line Whigs and Know-Nothings who did not feel they could support either the Democrats or the Republicans formed the Constitutional Union Party, which nominated John Bell and Edward Everett.

The election in Virginia was a close race between Bell and Breckinridge. The former won 74,481 votes to his opponent's 74,325. Douglas finished a distant third with 16,198 votes, and Lincoln, whose name was not even on the Virginia ballot, got only 1,187 votes. Nationally, Lincoln, with only 39.9 percent of the popular vote, was elected with more than twice as many electoral votes as Breckinridge, his nearest rival (180 to 72). Four days after the election, the South Carolina legislature called for a convention to consider removing the state from the Union. On December 20, they declared,

> *the people of the State of South Carolina in convention assembled, do declare and ordain…that the Union now subsisting between South Carolina and other States, under the name of "the United States of America," is hereby dissolved.*

Mississippi, Florida, Alabama, Georgia, Louisiana and Texas quickly followed suit. Representatives of all seven states met in Montgomery, Alabama, in February to declare the establishment of the Confederate States of America as a separate nation.

Virginia, while trying to maintain a position of neutrality between the Northern and Southern factions, called for a convention to meet in Richmond on February 13, 1861, to decide what course the state would take should the issue come to armed conflict. Loudoun voters selected two men, both loyal Unionists, to represent the county at this convention: respected attorney John Janney of Leesburg and gentleman farmer John Armistead Carter of Crednal. The first order of business was the election of John Janney as presiding officer. From the beginning, he set high goals for the convention:

> *It is our duty on occasions like this to elevate ourselves into an atmosphere in which party passions and prejudice cannot exist—to conduct all our deliberations with calmness and wisdom, and to maintain, with inflexible firmness, whatever position we may find it necessary to assume.*[12]

Even as Janney and Carter were arguing against secession in Richmond, a mass meeting was held in Leesburg in which one speaker after another called for the immediate severing of Virginia's connection with the Union. So thoroughly had the tide of public opinion shifted since the November election that the vote was virtually unanimous in passing resolutions calling upon the state convention to adopt an ordinance of secession. The convention's deliberations dragged on into April, with much of the debate centered on the question of whether secession must inevitably be followed by war. The majority of the delegates seemed to be confident that friendly relations between the North and South could continue even after the division of the country. They agreed, in view of the importance of the question, that whatever action the convention took would be submitted to the people of the state for ratification before it took effect.

The whole tone of the debate changed on April 12 when Confederate guns opened fire on the Union garrison of Fort Sumter in Charleston Harbor, South Carolina. Three days later, following the fort's surrender, Lincoln issued a call for seventy-five thousand volunteers to put down the rebellion in the Southern states, and even the most moderate Virginians had to admit that war was coming. Refusing to provide men to fight against

Crednal, the home of John Armistead Carter. *Photo by the author.*

the Southern Confederacy, the Virginia Convention passed an ordinance of secession on April 17, by a vote of eighty-eight to fifty-five, on the condition that it would be put to a vote by the people on May 23.

The people of Loudoun voted two to one to endorse the state convention's decision to take Virginia out of the Union. In only three of fifteen voting precincts, the Quaker communities of Waterford and Goose Creek (Waters precinct), and the German community of Lovettsville, the Unionists managed to achieve a majority. Everywhere else in the county, the vote overwhelmingly favored secession.

Precinct	For Secession	Against Secession
Aldie	54	5
Goreseville	117	19
Gum Spring	135	5
Hillsboro	84	38
Leesburg	400	22
Lovettsville	46	325
Middleburg	115	0

Precinct	For Secession	Against Secession
Mt. Gilead	102	19
Powells Shop	62	0
Purcellville	82	31
Snickersville	114	3
Union	150	0
Waterford	31	220
Waters	26	39
Whaleys	108	0
Total	**1,626**	**726**

Statewide, the vote for secession was even more lopsided, with 124,896 voters favoring the ordinance and only 20,390 opposing it. The local newspaper explained the drastic change in sentiment between February, when Loudoun County residents elected two Unionists to represent them at the state convention, and the May secession vote with a warning:

> *The unconstitutional usurpation of power by the government in Washington has wrought the change. Whether the 726 who opposed the action of the Convention designed to endorse the policy of the Republican administration we cannot pretend to assert; though that construction will be given their votes by those who desire a pretext for invading the South, it is certain.* [13]

Not everyone in the county was pleased with the vote. Rebecca Williams, a Quaker girl living in Waterford, wrote in her diary:

> *A large majority of the precinct* [voted] *for the Union but in other parts whole bodies of troops have been taken to the polls to vote for disunion and Union men have been intimidated &* [many] *have left the state…The prospect of dreadful times coming fills the heart with gloom.* [14]

It did not take the government in Washington long to react to Virginia's secession. Before dawn on May 24, the day after the vote, Union troops crossed the Potomac by way of the Long Bridge and the Aqueduct Bridge and occupied Alexandria and Arlington. Local militia withdrew ahead of them to avoid destructive fighting in the towns. Shortly after nine o'clock that morning, the last train from Alexandria arrived in Leesburg. It would be six long years before another train completed that trip.

Loudoun Prepares for War

Immediately on the arrival on Thursday [April 18] of the messenger from Gov. Letcher, the Loudoun Guard, Capt. Tebbs—the Loudoun Artillery, Capt. Rogers—and the Loudoun Cavalry, Capt. Shreve, were ordered to parade Friday morning at 10 o'clock, at which time the command turned out in large numbers. They were mustered into the service of the State and have been on drill every day since. The military spirit of our people is thoroughly aroused and some 25 or 30 new recruits have joined the service during the last day or two. These corps are composed of "good men and true" and in the language of an officer of the Guard if fighting must be done, they are ["spoilin'"] to take a stand.
—Democratic Mirror, *Wednesday morning, April 24, 1861*

The Loudoun Guard left town on April 27 to join the Sixth Battalion of Virginia Volunteers in Alexandria, and they were part of the command that abandoned the city when Union troops crossed the river. From Alexandria, they fell back to Manassas Junction where scattered companies were being collected and organized into regiments. The Guard became Company C of the new Seventeenth Virginia Infantry Regiment commanded by Colonel George H. Terrett, a former United States Marine. They had left home beneath colorful new flags, with martial music, the prayers of local clergymen and the patriotic words of their commanding officer echoing in their ears. They expected to be home in a matter of months, wearing the laurel wreath of victory and having done their part to secure the independence of the Confederate States. The terrible toll the war would exact on the county was mercifully hidden in the future. The Guard left Leesburg with sixty-six men present for duty. Only four would still be with the colors to surrender at Appomattox four years later.

Meanwhile, the recruiting and equipping of troops in Loudoun County continued. On May 1, little more than a week after the state seceded, the newspaper boasted, "Loudoun has already some 400 volunteers mustered into the service of the State." That same day the paper featured an announcement that William E. Harrison was recruiting for the Provisional Army of Virginia, and the editor encouraged, "Those of our young men not already enrolled…should make immediate application." At the same time,

Colonel Eppa Hunton, Eighth Virginia Infantry. *Courtesy of the USAMHI.*

Eppa Hunton, an attorney from neighboring Fauquier County and former member of the secession convention, was commissioned as colonel of state troops and he was sent to Leesburg to recruit the Eighth Virginia Infantry. His first act was to absorb the rest of Loudoun's militia companies into the new regiment.

The Provisional Army of Virginia was intended to be the regular army of the new Confederate States, made up of men and officers for whom the military was a profession, not a temporary occupation in a time of national emergency. By May 15, Harrison and James McCarty, another Loudoun County native and, like Harrison, a recent graduate of the Virginia Military Institute, had set up an office in the store of J.M. Drish, directly across King Street from the courthouse. Because they were competing for recruits with the militia companies, they were authorized by the state to offer a "premium of $2 to anyone who shall bring an accepted recruit to the office."[15] In the end, service in the regulars proved so unattractive to the volunteers that only five such regiments would see service in Virginia: two regiments of engineers, one infantry and two cavalry. Ultimately, McCarty left the Provisional Army for the volunteers, serving in Chew's battery of horse artillery and the Seventh and Eleventh Virginia Cavalry, while Harrison remained with the regulars in the First Infantry Battalion as a lieutenant of Confederate engineers.

In all, Loudoun County would contribute militia companies to seven different volunteer regiments, and individual soldiers to several more:

Loudoun Light Horse	Company H., First Virginia Cavalry
Loudoun Dragoons (The Dulany Troop)	Company A., Sixth Virginia Cavalry
Loudoun Cavalry	Company K., Sixth Virginia Cavalry
Captain Weems's Company	Company H., Eleventh Virginia Cavalry
White's Company (not recruited until 1862)	Company A., Thirty-fifth Virginia Cavalry
Hillsboro Border Guard	Company A., Eighth Virginia Infantry
Captain Mandley Hampton's Company	Company E., Eighth Virginia Infantry
Blue Mountain Boys	Company F., Eighth Virginia Infantry
Captain Simpson's Company	Company K., Eighth Virginia Infantry
Loudoun Guard	Company C., Seventeenth Virginia Infantry
Loudoun Artillery	Longstreet's Corps Artillery

In addition, Hunton recruited two more nonmilitia companies in Loudoun, making a total of six county companies in the Eighth Virginia. The balance of the regiment was made up of one company from Prince William County, two from Fauquier and one from Fairfax.

In those heady days immediately following secession, the problem was not a lack of men, but a lack of equipment for them. Colonel Edward McCrady of the First South Carolina Infantry recorded his own experience, which was typical of the experience of many officers, in a reunion address in 1886:

> *It is almost amusing now to recall the struggle it was to obtain the admission of a company, battalion or regiment into the Confederate army in the commencement of the war. The recruiting of the men was but a small part of the business. The most difficult was to furnish them with clothing and equipments. Fairs, and theatricals, and subscriptions, and all such devices were resorted to, and then, after having the rolls filled and the clothing provided, such as it was, the chances were that the government would refuse to receive them, because arms could not be procured…I had raised a battalion, and had them actually encamped and was providing their clothing, when, coming on to Richmond, I was informed the government would muster in only those for whom I could obtain arms, and as I could only obtain one hundred muskets—and those I almost stole—I had to disband the rest. The men I had in camp, and who were refused as volunteers, were afterwards conscripted.*[16]

To help alleviate the arms shortage that would plague the Confederacy throughout the war, the state ordered that all militia arms "not in the hand of Volunteer Companies," those held by militiamen who were too old for active service or those who had not yet enlisted in the new state regiments, be delivered to the colonels of local militia regiments. The merchants of Loudoun were quick to profit from the sudden need for uniforms and equipment. Even before Virginia's secession, Thomas Moralee of Leesburg was advertising,

> *I am prepared to furnish all types of Clothing at short notice. I am also prepared to furnish Swords, Hats, Epaulettes, and all kinds of Military Accoutrements. A full supply always of Military Buttons.*[17]

A week later, when the convention's secession vote became known, he started advertising, "Military Goods of all kinds furnished immediately."[18] Moralee's experience with providing uniforms for local soldiers could not have been entirely satisfactory to him. Within a month of these notices, he announced that all future sales would be cash only, with no credit extended even to "honest men."

As much as the newspaper boasted of the number of Loudoun men sent into the army, someone thought the pace of enlistments was too slow. Writing under the name "Sit Lux," this individual asked in the June 26, 1861 edition of the paper,

> *Where are our patriots...? Remember, Virginians! Those who do not volunteer promptly to fight with us, are very properly considered as operating in some way against us. Where is the Spirit of 76?*

There were a number of reasons why not everyone who was eligible to fight volunteered to do so. Chief among them were the pacifism and unionist sentiments of the Waterford, Lovettsville and Goose Creek communities; reluctance on the part of otherwise patriotic men to leave their farms and young families in planting season; and apathy on the part of men more interested in pursuing their own careers than in the fate of the Confederacy.

No one will ever know exactly how many men Loudoun County contributed to the cause because the enlistment records forwarded to Richmond were lost during the government's flight to North Carolina in 1865. Still, as James Head so eloquently expressed it,

> *It is certain that thousands of her sons espoused the cause of the Confederacy, hundreds died in its defense, and not a few, by their valor and devotion, won enduring fame and meritorious mention in the annals of their government.*[19]

The Dogs of War Let Loose

The first shots the residents of Loudoun County heard fired in anger were volleys of musketry exchanged between Union and Confederate pickets who were guarding fords on the Potomac River to the north and east of Leesburg. These were largely bloodless encounters that did little more than keep the people in a state of excitement and fear that one day the Yankees would cross the river in earnest. Aside from daily drills to teach his raw recruits the intricacies of battlefield maneuvers, Colonel Hunton's main preoccupation was with making preparations for Leesburg's defense. On May 24, he received orders from General Robert E. Lee, the commander of Virginia's army, to "destroy all the bridges of the Loudoun and Hampshire Railroad as far down towards Alexandria as possible" to hinder a possible Union drive from Alexandria toward Harpers Ferry.[20] The Union army had already destroyed the bridges as far west as Vienna, but Hunton completed the job from Leesburg to Hunter Mill. In addition, he made preparations to destroy the highway bridge across Goose Creek on short notice should the enemy advance.

Early in June, Colonel Thomas J. Jackson, who was commanding the Confederate troops in the Lower Shenandoah Valley, ordered the bridges across the Potomac at Harpers Ferry, Berlin (now Brunswick) and Point of Rocks burned. Hunton's job of defending the county, however, was still made difficult by numerous fords.

"Not a great while after I went to Leesburg," Hunton said,

> the United States forces appeared on the opposite side of the river, under the command of General C.P. Stone, of Washington City. This increased my labor in guarding the approaches to the county. I had to keep a guard at all the fords and ferries.

As part of the river guard, Hunton stationed a company of Maryland cavalry commanded by Captain George Gaither at Edwards Ferry, one of five major river crossings in the county (the other four being Conrad's Ferry, White's Ford, Point of Rocks and Berlin). Unfortunately, Gaither was not a very good officer. In Hunton's opinion, he was "excitable, emotional and unreliable in his reports." Late on the evening of June 8,

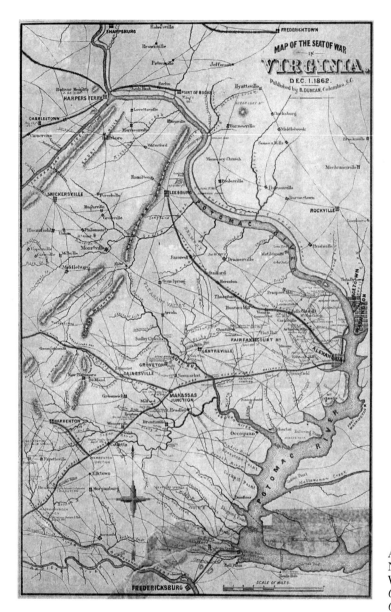

A map of the major
Northern Virginia Civil
War sites, 1861–1865.
*Courtesy of the Library of
Congress.*

Gaither frantically reported that a large Union force was crossing the river and that his men were about to be surrounded and captured. Before leaving Leesburg to check on the situation, Hunton ordered the destruction of the Goose Creek bridges and had his men set fire to most of the railroad cars at the station. Needless to say, the fires, drums and shouts of soldiers rushing off to reinforce the small Edwards Ferry detachment in the middle of the night caused quite a stir and more than a little panic in the town. To his disgust, when Hunton arrived, he found that "there had not been a single effort to cross; no preparation to cross, and evidently no idea on the part of General Stone of crossing the river."[21]

The *Democratic Mirror* lamented,

> *Saturday and Sunday last will long be remembered by the people of this section of the state as a period witnessing the destruction of certain public improvements, which had cost large sums of money, and labor, and works, in all probability, that the present generation will never see reconstructed. But as a military necessity seemed to demand their destruction, all good and loyal citizens will readily acquiesce in the movement.*[22]

Loudoun had heard its first gunfire and seen the first destruction of public property. There would be much worse to come in the years ahead.

July 1 saw the arrival of more soldiers when Major Nathan G. Evans and the Fourth South Carolina Infantry reached Leesburg. Colonel Hunton later wrote,

> *The South Carolinians boasted very strongly of what they were going to do. They said they had come there to fight the war and conquer peace. They did not want the Virginians to do any of the fighting, but just to stand back and look on and furnish them with bread and meat.*[23]

On July 15, the Carolinians returned to Manassas, and the Eighth Virginia followed them three days later. The armies were gathering for the first major battle of the war.

A detailed description of the battles outside of Loudoun County is not within the scope of this work. Suffice it to say that the Loudoun militia companies had their baptism of fire in the Confederate victory at First Manassas on July 21, 1861, and Eppa Hunton and the men of the Eighth Virginia were singled out for special praise in General P.G.T. Beauregard's after-action report to Richmond. The people of Loudoun County gained a new awareness of the cost of war, however, when the body of seventeen-year-old Virginia Military Institute (VMI) Cadet Charles R. Norris was brought home to Leesburg for burial in the Union Cemetery. Norris, who served as drillmaster to the Twenty-seventh Virginia Infantry, had been killed while leading one of several Confederate assaults on Henry Hill. He would be only the first of many battle casualties to be buried in the town.

Within a few days after the battle, Hunton and the Eighth Virginia returned to Loudoun County. They stopped for a time along the south bank of Goose Creek at Ball's Mill at a camp Hunton called "Camp Berkley" in honor of four brothers from Aldie who served in the Eighth Virginia. Shortly after the regiment returned to Leesburg, it was joined by the Thirteenth, Seventeenth and Eighteenth Mississippi regiments, a detachment of cavalry and one battery of the Richmond Howitzers. The four infantry regiments, the cavalry and the artillery formed a brigade under the command of the newly promoted Colonel Evans, who also had been singled out for praise for his actions at Manassas.

As summer passed into autumn, the men of the brigade alternated between drilling, picketing the river crossings and working on three forts Evans had ordered constructed to protect the town of Leesburg. The largest of the three forts, facing the Potomac River near Edwards Ferry, was Fort Evans, named for the commanding officer of the

Brigadier General Nathan "Shanks" Evans. *Courtesy of the USAMHI.*

brigade. Fort Johnston, named for General Joseph E. Johnston, was built on a hill a mile and a half west of town. Fort Beauregard sat on a hill east of town. Parts of two of the three forts still exist at this writing. Fort Beauregard was obliterated to make room for a housing development some years ago.

One of the more unusual events of the war took place on August 8 when the remaining railroad cars and the single engine the Confederates had taken from the Alexandria, Loudoun & Hampshire Railroad were moved by road from Leesburg to Piedmont (now Delaplane) and put into service on the Manassas Gap Railroad. Ida Powell Dulany of Upperville wrote the following day, "Yesterday all the cars from Leesburg passed our gate drawn by oxen and mules."[24] It must have been quite a spectacle for the residents of the county since Colonel Hunton reported that moving the engine alone "took twelve yoke of oxen."[25]

The remains of Fort Evans are still visible near Leesburg. *Photo by the author.*

Aside from occasional artillery fire from the north side of the Potomac and the infrequent report of a musket fired by a nervous or bored soldier on picket duty, life throughout that fall in Loudoun County was quiet. That blissful state of affairs changed drastically one October morning at a place called Ball's Bluff.

Ball's Bluff

"A Very Nice Little Military Chance"

by James A. Morgan III

The Battle of Ball's Bluff was an accident that resulted from a faulty intelligence report. It was not, as often is claimed, the result of a preplanned Federal attempt to take Leesburg.

In mid-October 1861, Captain Chase Philbrick's Company H, Fifteenth Massachusetts Volunteer Infantry was picketing Harrison's Island, which bisects the Potomac River at Ball's Bluff. On October 20, his division commander, Brigadier General Charles P. Stone, began maneuvering troops near the river so as to give the Confederates the impression that he was about to cross in force. Stone did this in response to a suggestion from Major General George McClellan that he should conduct "a slight demonstration" to see what effect it would have on the enemy.[26] McClellan's suggestion came out of his belief that the Confederates might have abandoned Leesburg, which, on October 16–17, they had done.

For about three weeks, Colonel Nathan "Shanks" Evans had been carefully watching the growing Union forces in the area, fearing that they might attempt to cut him off. His concerns began on October 3–5 when General Stone's division was reinforced by Colonel (and U.S. Senator) Edward D. Baker, whose large "California Brigade" boosted Stone's strength to approximately ten thousand men. Then, on October 9, Union Brigadier General George McCall crossed his twelve-thousand-man division into Virginia and established a camp at Langley, some twenty-five miles east of Leesburg.

Colonel Evans reasonably interpreted these movements as indicating a possible Union advance on Leesburg. The town was strategically significant as a regional transportation hub and because whoever controlled the fords and ferry sites in the vicinity controlled the invasion routes leading both north and south. Evans was legitimately concerned that his 2,800-man brigade, with no other Confederates in supporting distance, might prove too tempting a target to the nearby enemy.

Following some skirmishing upriver at Harpers Ferry that he apparently interpreted as the beginning of an attempted envelopment, Evans, without the permission of his superiors, abandoned Leesburg on the night of October 16. He moved his brigade southward and established a new defensive line behind Goose Creek, several miles from town, near Oatlands Plantation.

Brigadier General Charles P. Stone. *Courtesy of the USAMHI.*

General P.G.T. Beauregard was displeased when he heard of the move and he sent Evans a somewhat sarcastic message saying that he "wishe[d] to be informed of the reasons that influenced you to take up your present position, as you omit to inform him."[27] Evans took the hint and, by late on October 19, his brigade had returned to the town.

Not surprisingly, his departure had been observed by the Federals. General McClellan suspected a trap, thinking that Evans might be attempting to draw some of his forces forward in order to cut off and destroy them. He ordered General McCall to take his division on a reconnaissance in force as far as Dranesville, about halfway between Langley and Leesburg, and then to probe cautiously toward the latter town. McCall advanced to Dranesville on October 19, the very day of Evans's return to Leesburg.

On the morning of October 20, McCall was probing westward toward Leesburg. Evans was along another portion of Goose Creek, four miles east of Leesburg and some eight miles from McCall. With this in mind, McClellan ordered Stone to conduct the "slight demonstration" that led to Captain Philbrick's involvement.

Senator and Colonel Edward Baker. He was killed at Ball's Bluff. *Courtesy of the USAMHI.*

Carter's Mill, near Oatlands, circa 1890. *Courtesy of Oatlands, a National Trust site.*

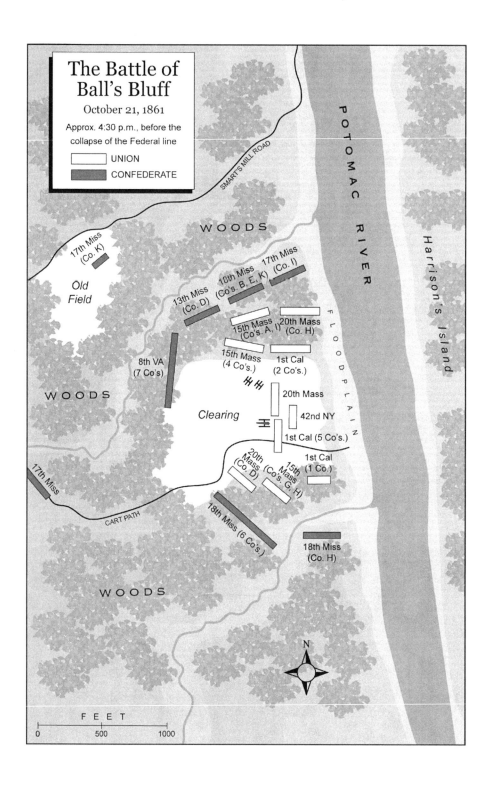

Map drawn by David Woodbury.

Ball's Bluff: "A Very Nice Little Military Chance"

By the evening of October 20, Stone's demonstration was over and the regiments that he had ordered to the river at Edwards Ferry (three miles south of Ball's Bluff) were on their way back to their camps for the night. He needed to know what effect his demonstration might have had, however, so he ordered Colonel Charles Devens to send a patrol across the river at Ball's Bluff.[28] Philbrick got the assignment partly because his company was already on Harrison's Island and partly because he had led a similar patrol on the evening of October 18 that had familiarized him with the area. On October 18, of course, the Confederates had not been there.

Around dusk, Philbrick and perhaps twenty volunteers used two small skiffs to cross quietly from the island to Ball's Bluff. The patrol moved downriver along the flood plain at the base of the bluff, and then up the bluff itself on a winding path that comes out just behind the current National Cemetery. Philbrick's men advanced inland along a small road. They crossed a ten- to twelve-acre clearing (later the focal point of the battle) and passed through some woods to the open fields that now are the site of the Potomac Crossing subdivision.

Lieutenant Church Howe described the patrol:

> We proceeded…three quarters of a mile or a mile from the edge of the river. We saw what we supposed to be an encampment. [There was] a row of maple trees; and there was a light on the opposite hill which shone through the trees and gave it the appearance of the camp. We were very well satisfied it was a camp.[29]

Captain Philbrick mistook the trees for tents. Without verifying what he thought he was seeing, however, he took his patrol back across the river and reported the presence of an unguarded camp. General Stone sensed what today would be called a target of opportunity. He called it "a very nice little military chance" and ordered a raid.[30] From this decision, based solely on Captain Philbrick's faulty report, came the Battle of Ball's Bluff. The raid on the camp often has been confused by historians with the "slight demonstration" of October 20, though the two are separate events. The demonstration, in fact, was ending as the Philbrick patrol was getting underway. The raid was organized after the patrol's return and only because of its faulty report. Preparations continued into the early hours of October 21.

The raid had the very limited purpose of attacking the alleged camp. But it appeared to the Confederates to be a more ambitious movement because, in addition to the crossing at Ball's Bluff, a small, diversionary crossing of cavalry was made downriver at Edwards Ferry. With McCall's division only a few miles away in Dranesville, and Yankees crossing the river at two points near Leesburg, the situation on the morning of October 21 must have appeared to Colonel Evans as the very envelopment he feared.

The Edwards Ferry crossing, however, was simply a small diversion in favor of Colonel Devens's raiding party. General Stone ordered Major John Mix to cross the river with thirty of his Third New York Cavalry troopers, advance toward Leesburg and attract attention to himself so that the raiding party upriver could conduct its raid and get back safely. Mix also was to scout between the river and the eastern approach to Leesburg (today's Route 7, the road on which McCall would come, should General McClellan order him to advance). Having accomplished these tasks, Mix was to withdraw to Maryland.[31]

McCall's instructions from General McClellan, however, would take him away from the fighting. He was under orders to complete his reconnaissance in force and return to Langley on the morning of October 21 (an important fact of which General Stone was unaware). Thus, none of the three Federal forces in the area that morning was there to attack the town. The assumption that they were has gained credence through repetition, and Ball's Bluff has consistently been misinterpreted as having resulted from Stone's implementation of a preexisting plan. The Federals all had limited missions and there was no plan. In fact, the only documented Union plan to take Leesburg was written by Stone in late January 1862, three months after the Battle of Ball's Bluff.

Colonel Devens shuttled his three-hundred-man raiding party across the river in three small boats carrying approximately thirty-five men per trip. In addition to the raiders from the Fifteenth Massachusetts, about a hundred men from the Twentieth Massachusetts followed in order to deploy on the bluff and cover the withdrawal of Devens's men following the raid.

Getting four hundred men across the river in three small boats, quietly and at night, was a difficult task made more so because heavy rains during the previous three weeks had caused the Potomac to rise to well above normal levels. The tricky crossing took most of the night. At around 6:00 a.m., as soon as it was light enough to see, Colonel Devens advanced on the "camp."[32]

He soon discovered the patrol's error and realized that his raiding party had nothing to raid. Had he then returned to the island, there would have been no battle. As commander on site, however, he used his discretionary authority and decided not to return right away. The morning was quiet and his force, as far as he could tell, remained unseen. Deploying his men along a tree line, he sent Lieutenant Howe to report to General Stone and request further instructions. Howe returned to the bluff, descended it, crossed the Virginia channel of the river to Harrison's Island and then crossed the island and the wider Maryland channel of the river. He then mounted a horse on the Chesapeake & Ohio Canal towpath and rode the three miles downriver to Edwards Ferry. He reported to Stone about 8:00 a.m. Reacting to Howe's new information, Stone ordered the remainder of the Fifteenth Massachusetts to join Devens with instructions that Devens was to advance his larger force toward Leesburg in what had now become an expanded reconnaissance mission. Howe went ahead of these reinforcements and brought Colonel Devens the new orders.

Unknown to General Stone, however, Devens was engaging the enemy even as Lieutenant Howe was making his initial report that everything was quiet. Pickets from Company K, Seventeenth Mississippi briefly had engaged a small patrol from the Twentieth Massachusetts near Smart's Mill, a mile or so north of Ball's Bluff, earlier in the morning. They then had sent word to Colonel Evans that Union troops were across the river at Ball's Bluff. Curiously, no one from the Twentieth Massachusetts bothered to inform Colonel Devens of the contact. We can only imagine his surprise when his scouts reported that Confederate troops were moving toward his position.

Ball's Bluff: "A Very Nice Little Military Chance"

Colonel Baker's command crossing from Harrison's Island to Ball's Bluff on October 21, 1861. *From John D. Baltz,* Colonel E.D. Baker's Defense in the Battle of Ball's Bluff, 1888.

Captain William Duff had forty-five men in his "Magnolia Guard." Upon hearing from the pickets, Duff mustered his company and moved southward in order to get between the Yankees and Leesburg. He encountered Devens's men not far from the home of the widowed Mrs. Margaret Jackson, near where the nonexistent camp was supposed to have been. Mrs. Jackson's home, though greatly altered, still stands today.

In the fields west of the Jackson house and north of the current subdivision, Duff's Mississippians engaged a portion of Devens's Massachusetts men. Devens had three hundred men with him but, not sure of the size of the Confederate force, he sent only Captain Philbrick's sixty-five-man Company H forward to meet the enemy. This initial skirmish lasted some fifteen to twenty minutes with the Southerners getting the best of it. They killed one, wounded nine and captured three of the Federals while suffering only three wounded men themselves. Both companies withdrew, and there began a three-hour lull while the events unfolded.

Shortly after Howe left General Stone with the instructions to turn the raid back into a recon, Colonel Edward Baker arrived at Edwards Ferry to find out what was going on. He had played no part in the events up to that point, except that Stone had ordered him to bring his brigade to Conrad's Ferry, just above Harrison's Island, in case it was needed.

Based on Howe's outdated information, Stone ordered Baker to evaluate the situation and either cross additional troops or recall those already in Virginia as he saw fit. Neither Stone nor Baker knew that fighting already had begun. Both were thinking only of an expanded reconnaissance toward Leesburg.

While on his way upriver shortly before 10:00 a.m., Baker met Lieutenant Howe, who was returning to Edwards Ferry with the new information about the skirmish. He told Howe that he was "going over immediately, with my whole force, to take command,"[33] but he did not actually do that. Instead, he ordered all the troops in the area to cross the river while he remained on the Maryland side and spent most of the next four hours looking for more boats. Not only did he not go to the battlefield himself, but he sent no orders and he put no one in overall command on the Virginia side.

There were two more skirmishes in the vicinity of the Jackson house. One occurred about 11:30 a.m. between the now 650-man Fifteenth Massachusetts and a mixed force of detached Mississippi infantry and Virginia cavalry companies totaling about the same number and now commanded by Lieutenant Colonel Walter Jenifer. The opposing forces were fairly evenly matched throughout the day, though each side reported being heavily outnumbered by the other.

A third skirmish took place about 1:00 p.m. after the Eighth Virginia (minus one company) arrived with just under four hundred men. Larger, but also indecisive, the skirmish was followed by another lull during which, around 2:00 p.m., Colonel Devens withdrew to the bluff, where he knew that he would have some help.

When Devens arrived at the bluff, he found Colonel Baker, who had just come across the river. Baker approved of Devens's withdrawal and ordered him to deploy on the right, perpendicular to the existing Federal line. This created a defensive position that would have looked from the bluff like a backwards *L*. The left wing faced west (the men's backs were to the bluff above the southward-flowing river) while Devens's men in the right wing faced south. Together they covered the road and the open field with a potentially deadly crossfire.

At about 3:00 p.m., Baker sent two companies of the First California (later redesignated the Seventy-first Pennsylvania) up the slope on his left front between today's cemetery and the parking lot in order to gauge the enemy's strength. This resulted in a clash between them and a portion of the Eighth Virginia near the site of the parking lot. From then on, there was almost continuous fighting until dark.

Both sides were hit hard in this brief but intense encounter. The Californians fell back to the main Union line, but the clash, combined with a misunderstood order to withdraw and regroup, caused the companies of the Eighth Virginia that were farthest to the right to break and run. Colonel Eppa Hunton deserves great credit for preventing the spread of what might have become a disastrous panic. He moved the Eighth to a large field near the Jackson house and spent the next ninety minutes to two hours reorganizing and getting it back into the fight. Most of the men who had fled did return eventually, and the unit was involved in one more charge later in the day.

When Hunton withdrew, the Eighteenth Mississippi took his place in the line and almost immediately advanced across the field, marching right between the two wings of the Federal position. Colonel Erasmus Burt's tactical error here probably resulted from

A contemporary depiction of the death of Colonel Baker. *Courtesy of the Library of Congress.*

his not being able to see the Federal right, as those men were under the cover of woods and sloping ground while the left was in the open. Burt marched directly into what Confederate soldier Elijah White later called "the best directed & most destructive single volley I saw during the war."[34] Burt was one of the casualties. Shot through the hip, he was taken into Leesburg where he died on October 26.

The Mississippians quickly withdrew and split into two battalions. One moved to flank the Federals on the left and the other to do the same on the right. This created a wide gap in the Confederate line—roughly near the location of today's parking lot—that the Federals failed to exploit due to Colonel Baker's decision to remain on the defensive. The gap eventually was filled by the Seventeenth Mississippi.

Federal troops retreat from Ball's Bluff into the Potomac River. *Courtesy of the Library of Congress.*

From this point, the fighting was a swirl of company or battalion actions. Heavy skirmishing persisted on the Confederate left all afternoon, but the heaviest fighting was on their right. The Mississippians, who had moved into the ravines on the right, attacked at least five times during the afternoon and were repulsed each time. It most likely was during the last of those assaults between 4:30 and 5:00 p.m. that Colonel Baker was killed, though there is no historically definitive account of his death. Baker, one of President Lincoln's closest friends, is the only U.S. senator to have been killed in battle.

Command of the Union troops fell to Colonel Milton Cogswell of the Forty-second New York. Colonel Devens and Colonel William R. Lee of the Twentieth Massachusetts both urged a retreat, but Cogswell wanted first to attempt to break out of the constricted position by advancing, to give his force room to maneuver and better use its artillery.

Veterans of the Fifteenth Massachusetts Infantry visit the Ball's Bluff battlefield in 1886, twenty-five years after the fighting there. *Courtesy of Jeff Randolph, Northern Virginia Regional Park Authority.*

Earlier in the day, he had urged this course on Baker, but Baker had refused, preferring to fight a defensive battle.

Cogswell's breakout, a desperation move to be conducted by worn-out men who were short on water and ammunition, never really got organized. Shortly before dusk, the Seventeenth Mississippi, comprising six to seven hundred fresh troops with full cartridge boxes, arrived on the field and effectively sealed the fate of the Federals. Supported by the Eighteenth, and possibly by a company of the Thirteenth Mississippi and some dismounted Virginia cavalrymen, the Seventeenth advanced and broke the Union line.

The panic-stricken Federals rushed down the steep slope at the southern end of Ball's Bluff all the way to the river. Many of them drowned or were shot as they attempted to swim to Harrison's Island. Others took cover at the base of the bluff and later surrendered. More than 50 percent of the Union force became casualties: 223 were killed, 226 wounded and 553 taken prisoner out of a total force of 1,700. The *Official Records (OR)* state that 49 Union soldiers were killed in the battle, but that figure, often cited in secondary accounts because of its appearance in the *OR*, is wrong. Regimental returns, medical records and the many reports of bodies washing ashore along the

Potomac in the days following the battle provide the higher, more accurate numbers. The Confederates, who also put about 1,700 men into the fight, suffered fewer than 40 killed, 110 wounded and 3 captured.

The primary responsibility for the Federal disaster must belong to Baker. As commander on the field, he made some unfortunate decisions with regard to the crossing and the deployment of his men. The Southern command structure, however, also had problems as the ranking officer on the field changed several times during the day. Captain Duff was succeeded by Lieutenant Colonel Jenifer, who was succeeded by Colonel Hunton until the Eighth Virginia fell into disarray. Colonel Erasmus Burt of the Eighteenth Mississippi briefly commanded until he was wounded and taken from the field, leaving Jenifer again as the senior officer for a time. On Hunton's return, he commanded the Virginians and the detached Mississippi companies on the left. Colonel Winfield Scott Featherston of the Seventeenth Mississippi arrived and commanded his regiment and the detached Mississippi companies on the right.

Hunton led one more charge on the left that overran two Federal mountain howitzers and then he withdrew his regiment. Shortly thereafter, Featherston led the climactic assault that finally drove the Union troops into the river. He was in overall command of the Confederates on the field at the end of the day.

Ball's Bluff was a minor affair and was soon overshadowed by larger, bloodier battles. In 1866, General Stone described it as being "about equal to an unnoticed morning's skirmish on the lines before Petersburg at a later period of the war." In late 1861, though, it was a fight of considerable significance.

Stone, despite being publicly exonerated by General McClellan, saw his career ruined. Six weeks after the battle, political pressures increased when the Joint Committee on the Conduct of the War was organized and Congress became deeply involved in all war-related activities from then on. On the military side, the victory was celebrated by Southerners as a sign of things to come. For the defeated Yankees, however, the name "Ball's Bluff" became a curse, and they no doubt feared that the Southerners' predictions were right.

Gateway to War

Shortly after the Battle of Ball's Bluff, Colonel Evans was promoted to brigadier general and sent to command the First Military District of South Carolina. His replacement in command of the Confederate troops in Loudoun was Brigadier General Daniel Harvey Hill, a graduate of the West Point Class of 1842 and brother-in-law to "Stonewall" Jackson. Hill was an outspoken South Carolinian whose lack of tact would get him into serious trouble later in the war, but he was well suited to his new command. With an administrator's organization skills and a trained artillerist's eye for terrain, he strengthened the forts around Leesburg and had his men begin working on a strong network of earthworks between the town and the Potomac crossings.

Facing him across the river in Harpers Ferry was Colonel John W. Geary of the Twenty-eighth Pennsylvania Volunteer Infantry, a giant of a man for the time, who stood six feet six inches tall and weighed 260 pounds. Geary knew Loudoun well; he ran the Potomac Iron Company, which had extensive mineral properties in the county, before the war. Wounded five times in the Mexican War, Geary had served as San Francisco's first postmaster, and later as the first mayor of the city, before he accepted an appointment as territorial governor of Kansas. He was an ardent abolitionist and Republican, and he harbored little sympathy for Southern slaveholders, as the people of Loudoun County would soon learn.

Throughout the winter of 1861–62, the armies sat quietly on the banks of the Potomac. Pickets frequently declared truces of their own and met to exchange Southern tobacco for Northern coffee and newspapers—items in increasingly short supply in Confederate territory. (The Loudoun newspaper had ceased publication in December, citing a shortage of paper as the cause.) George McClellan, who had taken command of the Union army after the disaster at First Manassas, spent the winter in heavily fortified positions around Washington, drilling new volunteers and organizing them into a force of more than a hundred thousand men. Meanwhile, Joseph Johnston had his Confederate army camped around Manassas. On the Shenandoah Valley side of the Blue Ridge Mountains, Union General Nathaniel Banks kept watch over the valley, while the ever-aggressive Stonewall Jackson defended Winchester by means of a midwinter campaign into the mountains of what is now West Virginia.

General John White Geary. As colonel of the Twenty-eighth Pennsylvania Infantry, Geary led the first of many Union occupations of Loudoun County. *Courtesy of the USAMHI.*

BATTLE OF DRANESVILLE

In late December, there was excitement caused by a chance encounter between Union and Confederate foraging parties at Dranesville, just across the county line between Loudoun and Fairfax. The battle was a classic meeting engagement, with neither side expecting to fight when they met at the intersection of Old Georgetown Road (now Georgetown Pike) and the Leesburg Pike (Route 7) on December 20.

The Confederate forces, commanded by Brigadier General J.E.B. Stuart, included four infantry regiments, Cutts's Battery of Sumter Flying Artillery and a 150-man cavalry detachment escorting virtually every wagon in Johnston's army. The Union forces, commanded by Brigadier General E.O.C. Ord, consisted of five regiments of Pennsylvania Infantry, a squadron of cavalry and Captain Easton's four-gun Battery A, Pennsylvania Light Artillery.

A 1953 picture of the Broad Run Tollhouse on the Leesburg Pike (Route 7). *Courtesy of Muriel Spetzman.*

Stuart's plan was to have his wagons gather forage from Northern sympathizers between Dranesville and Broad Run while his covering force deployed astride the turnpike to protect them from Union patrols. Ord had received word that Confederate cavalry were intimidating Unionists in the Dranesville area, and he was assigned to punish the Rebel raiders while collecting a supply of forage from secessionists in the area.

Ord's leading elements, the cavalry, Easton's Battery and an infantry screen made up of the First Pennsylvania Rifle (Bucktails) and the Ninth Pennsylvania Infantry, reached Dranesville around noon, scattering the small Confederate cavalry picket there. They had been in the area for about an hour when Stuart's cavalry was spotted coming out of the woods south and southeast of the village. Colonel Kane, who was commanding the Bucktails, ordered his regiment to the high ground on the north side of the pike, placing one company "in a gully or trench parallel to the road" to support Easton's guns. Easton's position was just east of the present-day driveway to the Dranesville Church of the Brethren, which was built after the war.

Because the Sixth, Ninth and Twelfth Pennsylvania regiments already had passed the intersection heading west toward Liberty Meetinghouse (now Dranesville United Methodist Church), Ord quickly ordered them to countermarch to avoid being struck in the flank and rear. With his command united at the highway intersection, he ordered Easton to engage the enemy's guns. In the exchange of artillery fire, a shell from one of Easton's twenty-four-pounders struck a Confederate caisson, which exploded and killed several men and horses.

Stuart, meanwhile, positioned his troops as they arrived on the field. Four companies of the Eleventh Virginia Infantry were deployed across the Centreville Road (now Reston Avenue) and two companies to either side. Minutes later, the Sixth South Carolina arrived and went into line to the left of the road. Behind it was the Tenth Alabama. When the First Kentucky came on the scene, Stuart briefly considered holding it in reserve, but seeing the length of the Union line, he decided to deploy it to the left of the South Carolinians. Almost immediately, the Kentuckians, confused while moving through heavy timber, began exchanging volleys with the South Carolinians before officers of both regiments were able to stop the firing and correct alignments.

The battle began in earnest when Stuart ordered his right to advance at almost the same instant Ord put his left into motion. The First Kentucky was hit in the flank by the Ninth Pennsylvania. Then the Virginia and Alabama regiments came under heavy fire from Pennsylvanians, who were sheltered behind brick buildings on the far side of the road (where the North Point Fire Station now stands). For nearly half an hour, Union and Confederate forces traded fire, with the Southerners getting the worst of it. Easton's guns continued to pound the Sumter battery. Stuart admitted in his report that every shot seemed to hit a man, horse or gun.

After deciding that his wagons had had enough time to make their escape, Stuart withdrew behind a screen of smoke and heavy timber. Although he later claimed to have been greatly outnumbered, the forces were almost evenly matched. Ord had five regiments to Stuart's four, but he held half of the Tenth Pennsylvania and all of his cavalry in reserve. While the number of casualties was slight in comparison to the losses at Manassas and Ball's Bluff, losses reported by both commanders show a total of 194 Confederates killed or wounded, and 68 Federals. Despite the small numbers engaged, however, Northern newspapers hailed the battle as a great victory—the first won by Union troops on Virginia's soil. By the time the war ended four years later, Dranesville would rate barely a footnote in the state's history; but in 1861, it was big news on both sides of the line.[35]

THE FIRST INVASION

The first Union occupation of any portion of Loudoun County began on February 24, 1862, when Colonel Geary started moving his regiment to Lovettsville from Harpers Ferry. Because this was the strongly unionist "German Settlement," the Northerners were greeted as liberators. Geary reported,

> *A general expression of loyalty has transpired in this county, and joyous manifestations of fealty to the old Government have greeted us, and hundreds of the residents have come forward and claimed our protection from the dominion and obnoxious restrictions placed upon them by the rebel soldiery.*[36]

With his artillery posted on Short Hill Mountain and with a strong defensive line to the south and east of town, Geary was in an excellent position to stop frequent Confederate raids on the Baltimore & Ohio Railroad (B&O), just across the river.

In March, McClellan started moving his army by water to the James River Peninsula below Richmond. To counter this, Johnston withdrew his army from Manassas and headed south. Once they moved out, the Loudoun position was no longer tenable, and Hill made preparations to follow. Geary claimed that his arrival kept Confederate cavalry from burning Lovettsville and Waterford. More likely, he kept them from burning haystacks and granaries, which they were doing to deny vital supplies to the Yankees. Hill did not exactly practice a "scorched earth" policy, but his order for the destruction of crops introduced Loudoun County civilians to the "hard hand of war." They would see much more extensive destruction before the war was over.

LOUDOUN'S UNSUNG HERO

As soon as word came that the Confederates were abandoning Loudoun, Asa Rogers, the presiding justice of the county court, ordered twenty-eight-year-old George K. Fox Jr., clerk of the court,

> *to remove the county records to a place of safety and to use his discretion for their preservation. Pursuant to these instructions, Mr. Fox loaded the records into a large wagon and with them drove south to Campbell County.*[37]

For three years, Fox moved the records from place to place as each of his sanctuaries became threatened by Union raiding parties. Eventually, the war ended and new county officers and justices were elected. Their first order of business in July 1865 was to

> *order that George K. Fox, Junior, as Clerk of this Court, having removed from this County the records of the Court under an order heretofore made, he is now ordered to return the records to the Clerk's Office of this Court as soon as possible at the expense of the County.*[38]

The newspaper reported on August 9, 1865, that

> *George K. Fox, Junior, Esquire, late Clerk of the Court, reached home Friday from the Devil's Kitchen with the Records of the County which were removed more than three years ago by Order of the Court. They were returned in good condition without the loss of a single paper, or so much as the rubbing of the bindings of the books.*

Thanks to Mr. Fox, who neither visited his home nor saw his family for three years, Loudoun County now has a more complete set of public records than any Virginia county whose courthouse was occupied by Union troops during the war. Because he had held public office under the Confederate government, Fox was disenfranchised at the end of the war, and Charles P. Janney was elected in his place. So strong was the friendship between the two men that Janney appointed Fox as his assistant. Fox was later reelected clerk and held the job until his death at the age of forty in 1872.[39]

GEARY IN LOUDOUN

Before entering Leesburg, Colonel Geary moved into Fort Johnston, which his men immediately renamed "Fort Geary." After placing two cannon in a position "commanding the city," he then occupied "the court-house, post-office, bank, and all public buildings, and Forts Beauregard and Evans."[40] The Pennsylvanians spent only a short time in Leesburg before heading to Middleburg, which they reached around noon. The Confederates they encountered there, reported by Geary to be "200 cavalry and 200 infantry," were actually Captain Elijah White and seventy or so men of his Ranger Company. Loudoun County witnessed one of the war's "firsts" when Geary's men fired shots from their "Union Repeating Guns" (better known as coffee-mill guns) at White's men. This was the first use of a machine gun in combat.[41]

Geary boasted,

> *We have made an impression upon* [the people] *by a respect for property and proper exhibition of decorum, which they have been educated to suppose was foreign to us, as we were designated as ruthless pillagers.*[42]

Ida Dulany might have disagreed with him. Her journal entry for March 19 included the following:

> *At Mr. Bolling's they have behaved shamefully, insulting him, and treating him so that he is almost deranged from indignation. They have taken from him every horse, all his provender, and some of his servants…In a few moments…we heard reports of a gun and I found another party were shooting my cattle. They shot about forty times and finally ran the whole drove off the place. Then I heard firing in another direction and found they were shooting my turkeys. They are by no means good shots as with all their firing they only killed four steers and two turkeys. The whole party soon came in the yard…*[T]*hey insisted they had a right to everything they wanted because* [my husband] *was in arms for the South.*

Geary did not stay long in Loudoun on this first trip into the county. After only a few days in Upperville, he was ordered to move to The Plains in Fauquier County to begin repairing the Manassas Gap Railroad. Shortly afterward, he was ordered to return to Harpers Ferry. Stonewall Jackson's campaign in the Shenandoah Valley convinced the army's commanders in Washington that they needed all the troops they could get between the Lower Valley and Washington, DC. For a little more than a month, Loudoun was once again largely Yankee-free.

Colonel Elijah V. White, the hero of Ball's Bluff and the commander of the Thirty-fifth Virginia Cavalry. *Courtesy of the Northern Virginia Regional Park Authority.*

Two Men on Opposite Sides

Although the Civil War in Loudoun County never approached the level of brutality experienced in Missouri and Kansas, the conflict was very much a "brother's war" that divided families and pitted longtime friends against one another on the battlefield. The fratricidal nature of the conflict was typified by the history of two military units, one Union and one Confederate, both raised largely in Loudoun County.

The Confederates scored first in the recruiting competition in northwestern Loudoun when Elijah V. "Lige" White, a Poolesville native living near Leesburg, received permission to raise an independent cavalry company for "service on the border." Throughout the war, he drew his recruits mostly from Loudoun, Frederick, Page and Shenandoah Counties in Virginia and from Montgomery and Frederick Counties in Maryland.

White originally enlisted in a company of Rangers recruited by Angus MacDonald in the Lower Shenandoah Valley. MacDonald was a rather unorthodox West Point graduate who believed tomahawks were more appropriate weapons for cavalrymen than sabers. MacDonald also believed that horsemen should strike without warning and retire swiftly in small groups rather than in the massed ranks so popular with officers trained in Napoleonic tactics and with artists who specialized in painting heroic battlefield scenes. Because he was sixty-two years old when he raised his company, MacDonald soon relinquished his command to a younger, if equally unorthodox, cavalryman, Lieutenant Colonel Turner Ashby.[13] Lige White was still a member of "Ashby's Rangers" when he served as a volunteer scout and courier for Colonel Eppa Hunton during the Battle of Ball's Bluff. As one of the heroes of the Confederate victory, he soon gained permission to raise his own cavalry company.

Loudoun's only Union unit came into existence late in 1862 when Samuel C. Means, a Quaker and miller from Waterford, was offered a commission to raise an independent cavalry company among loyal refugees in Maryland who fled Virginia to escape persecution at the hands of Confederate authorities. It did not take Means long to raise the first of two small companies mustered into Federal service on June 20, 1862, as the Loudoun Independent Rangers.[14] Despite the pacifism of their religion, a number of

Loudoun's Quakers enlisted in the new unit. From the moment the news of the new regiment got out, they were despised by Loudoun's secessionists and condemned as traitors by Virginia and Confederate authorities. Almost immediately, a bounty was offered for the dead body of Means, and Lige White adopted the destruction of the hated Union company as his personal crusade.

The parallels between the Loudoun Rangers and the Confederate battalion that later took the name "White's Comanches" were striking, but not surprising in view of their common origin. The first two companies of both units were recruited in the same part of Loudoun County, and many of the same surnames appear on both muster rolls. Relations between the two bands were particularly hostile because the men knew each other and were, in a number of cases, related by marriage or by blood. Both units were created for "service on the border," and both struggled throughout the war to maintain their individual identities.

In White's case, his men were regularly brigaded with the cavalry of the Army of Northern Virginia as the Thirty-fifth Virginia Cavalry. The first order assigning the Thirty-fifth to a regular cavalry brigade was met with such resentment and hostility that White barely managed to avoid a mutiny in one of his companies. Captain George Chiswell's Company B, composed mostly of Marylanders, claimed that, as citizens of a state that had not seceded from the Union, they could fight when and where they chose, and owed no particular allegiance to the Confederate States of America. White, himself a Maryland native, managed to convince them to stay with him and make the best of whatever opportunities came along to attack and discomfit the conquerors of their native soil.

Means was his own worst enemy when it came to preserving the organizational integrity of the Loudoun Rangers. Because he had received his commission directly from the secretary of war, he maintained the he was under no obligation to follow the orders of his superior officers in the Union army. He jealously asserted his right to confine his company's operations to those portions of Maryland and Virginia that bordered the Potomac River between Harpers Ferry and Great Falls. Eventually, Means would resign his commission after refusing to obey an order transferring his command to West Virginia and merging it with the Third West Virginia Cavalry. (By the time Secretary of War Edwin Stanton resolved the dispute in his favor, Means had already left the army.)[45]

That still lay in the future, however, on an August day in 1862 when about half the men of the new Loudoun Rangers (twenty-four men and officers) made their camp in the Baptist Meetinghouse in Waterford. Early on the morning of the twenty-seventh, Lige White led his men across open country, avoiding the Union pickets on the roads leading into the town. His objective, he said, was "to whip Means and his men, and that no matter how much force they had, he intended to do it."

Shortly before dawn, he sent twenty dismounted men under the command of Captain J.W. Randolph of the Twelfth Virginia Cavalry with orders to drive the Yankees away from the brick church so they could be easily captured by the rest of the command, which remained mounted in the roadway. Unfortunately, Randolph's men began firing too soon, and they merely drove the Rangers into the church after severely wounding

Lieutenant Luther Slater, the Union commanding officer. For the next ninety minutes, the two parties exchanged indecisive volleys, until both sides were running low on ammunition. White considered withdrawing from the fight, but he was loath to leave without at least capturing the Rangers' horses, which were tied in the churchyard. Luckily, from his perspective, many of the Union troopers were wounded, and their ammunition was almost exhausted.

White made two attempts to convince the Rangers to surrender, promising to parole all prisoners and allow the officers to keep their personal side arms. Finally, drillmaster Charles Webster, who was commanding in place of the wounded Lieutenant Slater, surrendered the Rangers. The brief surrender ceremony in which the Rangers who were able to stand formed a line and gave up their arms presented a curious spectacle. "Many," said Frank Myers of the Thirty-fifth Virginia, "were old friends and had been schoolboys with some of White's men." One sergeant of the Thirty-fifth, William Snoots, loudly demanded to be allowed to kill one of the Union prisoners, his own brother Charles. Had he not been restrained, his actions might have set a tone of brutality and disregard for the laws of war that would have made Loudoun County a much bloodier and more brutal battleground than it was. To the good fortune of every man who fought in Loudoun for the remainder of the war, however, Charles Snoots was paroled and allowed to march north with his comrades.[16]

A 1905 photograph of the Waterford Baptist Church (left), the site of the August 1862 fight between White's Company and the Independent Loudoun Rangers. *Courtesy of the Thomas Balch Library.*

White's captures that day included fifty-six horses, complete with saddles and bridles, and more than a hundred revolvers and carbines (weapons in short supply in the Confederacy). He captured and paroled a total of thirty soldiers and officers. His cost was one man killed, one mortally wounded and several others slightly wounded. The Rangers suffered one man killed, one mortally wounded, eight men with lesser wounds and the entire command captured. The prize White most coveted escaped him, however. Means had been spending the night with his family rather than in the church with his men. Hearing the first shots of the attack, he quickly mounted his horse and made his escape.

The Rangers and the Comanches clashed many more times, although the Thirty-fifth Virginia was only rarely in Loudoun as an intact unit for the rest of the war. Individuals and small detachments returned to the "border" as often as possible. On September 1, 1862, the Rangers surprised a detachment of the Thirty-fifth Virginia at Hillsboro, driving the Confederates from the town and capturing two of them. The next day, they were less successful when they ran into the Second Virginia Cavalry about a mile north of Leesburg. Their ebbing fortunes saw them only a short time later in the garrison at Harpers Ferry when Colonel Dixon Miles decided to surrender his command to General Stonewall Jackson. The Rangers, however, were among the cavalrymen who managed to escape the town before its surrender and they made their way into Pennsylvania while Harpers Ferry and its twelve thousand defenders fell, and the bloody Battle of Antietam was fought behind them.

That the Loudoun Rangers never managed to recruit enough men to become a battalion, let alone a full regiment, is probably because most of Loudoun's Unionists were also ardent pacifists. The Quakers and Brethren were excellent farmers whose thrift and industry fed and clothed the fighting men of both sides for three long years, but they were poor candidates for the recruiting officer because of their religious beliefs. Thus, the Rangers never numbered more than two companies.

They suffered their final indignity only three days before General Robert E. Lee surrendered his Army of Northern Virginia to General U.S. Grant. While camped at Keyes Switch on the B&O Railroad, just west of Harpers Ferry, the command was surprised by Mosby's Rangers and captured down to the last of their sixty-five men and eighty-one horses. Their final battle ended with the same result as their first. When Army Chief of Staff Winfield Scott Hancock learned of their fate, he is said to have laughed loudly and said, "Well, that's the last of the Loudoun Rangers."[47]

White's Comanches, on the other hand, served loyally as part of the famed Laurel Brigade for the duration of the war. The regiment took part in most of the cavalry actions from Brandy Station to Appomattox, including several foraging raids into West Virginia and Wade Hampton's "Beefsteak Raid" during the Siege of Petersburg. With the mortal wounding of General James Dearing at High Bridge (which was fought the same day the Loudoun Rangers surrendered to Mosby), Lige White became the last commanding officer of the Laurel Brigade. Three days later, he and his men took part in the cavalry's breakout from Appomattox Court House and disbanded rather than surrender.

To Antietam

THE MARYLAND CAMPAIGN OF 1862

The day after Lige White attacked the Loudoun Rangers in Waterford, Stonewall Jackson started the three-day fight that would be known as the Battle of Second Manassas. At the conclusion of that conflict, the Union army retreated to strong defensive positions around Washington to lick its wounds. Lee's Army of Northern Virginia pursued them as far as Fairfax before turning northwest toward Leesburg. In preparation for the move, Lee had Stuart send Colonel Thomas Munford with his Second Virginia Cavalry into Loudoun County to see how many Union troops he might encounter along the way.

BATTLE OF MILE HILL

Reaching town shortly before noon on September 2, Munford found Leesburg occupied by the Loudoun Rangers and about 150 men of Major Henry Cole's "Maryland Cavalry," a battalion made up of Union men from Western Maryland and Virginia. It took about half an hour for him to scout the situation and send a portion of his command charging into town while the rest waited in ambush in the woods along the road to Point of Rocks. As the Yankees fled to the north, Munford, joined by Captain White and his men, managed to surround them between Mile Hill and the Big Spring on the Carolina Road. The fight started near the present intersection of the Route 15 Bypass and Business 15 and moved southwest across Morven Park and Ida Lee Park. By the time the last of Cole's men escaped, Munford had suffered two men killed and five wounded, while Cole and the Loudoun Rangers together saw eleven killed, nine too badly wounded to be moved and forty-seven captured.[48] The remnants of the two Union cavalry units withdrew all the way to Harpers Ferry, where they would be part of the cavalry breakout led by Colonel Arno Voss of the Twelfth Illinois Cavalry before the Federal garrison there surrendered.

The day after the Mile Hill fight, Lee wrote to President Jefferson Davis from his camp near Dranesville:

The present seems to be the most propitious time since the commencement of the war for the Confederate Army to enter Maryland...I therefore determined...to draw the troops into Loudoun, where forage and some provisions can be obtained, menace their possession of the Shenandoah Valley, and, if found practicable, to cross into Maryland. The purpose, if discovered, will have the effect of carrying the enemy north of the Potomac.[49]

LEE IN LEESBURG

Lee and Jackson reached Leesburg on September 3. Lee was riding in an ambulance because, a few days earlier, he had been standing by his horse when Traveler shied at something and pulled the general to the ground. Putting out his hands to break his fall, Lee broke a bone in one wrist and severely sprained the other. His host in Leesburg was Mr. Henry Harrison, who owned a fine, large house on North King Street (205 North King Street, now known as the Glendfidditch House). After conferring with Jackson about his plans for the campaign in Maryland, Lee walked a short distance from the Harrison home to pay a social call on John Janney, who had presided over Virginia's secession convention.

While in Leesburg, Lee reorganized the transport branch of his army, reducing the number of wagons and sending broken-down teams of horses and mules away to be given a chance to recover. Likewise, sick and wounded men were sent to Winchester to await the army's return. Lee also consolidated his artillery batteries to be sure there were enough good teams to pull all the guns he was taking across the river with him. Meanwhile, Jackson rose early on the morning of September 4 to make a personal survey of the Potomac fords to determine the best place for the army to cross into Maryland. Although some accounts say they crossed at Edwards's and Noland's ferries, strong evidence suggests that the largest part of the army crossed at White's Ford, not far from the mouth of the Monocacy River, where the river is broad and only a few feet deep.[50]

George Neese, an artilleryman in Chew's battery of horse artillery, reported,

Thousands of soldiers camped around Leesburg this evening, and all seem to be in joyous gayety, caused, I suppose, by bright anticipations of crossing the Potomac and entering Maryland. As I am writing I hear soldiers shouting, huzzahing all around us. Just now a brass band has struck up, which helps to swell the cheer of the merry throng...It was midnight when we left the Southern Confederacy...forded the Potomac, and landed in the United States, Montgomery County, Maryland.[51]

Brigadier General John G. Walker returned to Loudoun County after only a few days in Frederick. He was sent to lead one portion of Jackson's three-prong advance on the Union garrison at Harpers Ferry. Walker and his men slowly hauled a battery of artillery up the eastern slope of the Loudoun Heights and had them in position to shell the town when Jackson began his assault on September 14. After the Union surrender, Walker's brigade crossed the river to rejoin the army near Sharpsburg for the bloody Battle of Antietam.

Alfred Waud's sketch of Union pickets watching the Confederate army cross the Potomac River at White's Ford on their way to Antietam. *Courtesy of the Library of Congress.*

KILPATRICK SHELLS LEESBURG

On September 17, as the Battle of Antietam was being fought in Sharpsburg, Lieutenant Colonel Hugh Judson Kilpatrick, Second New York Cavalry, led ten companies of Union cavalry and an artillery battery northwest from Fairfax to Leesburg. Despite finding the bridge across Goose Creek burned, they brushed aside a small Confederate cavalry picket and advanced on the town. The total Confederate force there consisted of Company A, Sixth Virginia Cavalry, and about forty Mississippi infantrymen under the command of Captain Tully Gibson, the provost marshal. In addition, there were a number of sick and wounded men being cared for in local homes. Kilpatrick, in typical fashion, reported that the Confederate force facing him consisted of two hundred cavalry and five hundred infantrymen.[52]

Gibson and the Sixth Virginia were in the process of withdrawing out the west side of town when Captain White arrived with about thirty of his men and persuaded them not to leave without a fight. Returning to their former positions, they saw Kilpatrick had unlimbered his battery and was preparing to shell the town. According to Frank Myers,

Brigadier General Hugh Judson Kilpatrick. *Courtesy of the Library of Congress.*

"shrieking shells came crashing through the walls and roofs," while Kilpatrick claimed to have fired "a few shells…over the town."[53] After firing a few rounds from his cannon, Kilpatrick sent the Tenth New York Cavalry charging down Market Street. As White prepared to meet the Yankees with a countercharge, he was wounded by a shot fired by one of the Confederate infantrymen. When his men retreated with their wounded captain to Hamilton, the infantry followed, leaving Leesburg to Kilpatrick. Colonel J.M. Davies, Kilpatrick's brigade commander, admitted to suffering two men killed, twelve wounded and one missing in the brief exchange of fire. Neither White nor Gibson made a record of Confederate losses.

Not long after this small affair, the Confederate army returned from Maryland by way of the Shenandoah Valley while the Union army rested in Maryland, and a period of calm returned to Loudoun County for several weeks.

STUART'S CHAMBERSBURG RAID

On October 10, Jeb Stuart, along with eighteen hundred cavalrymen and Pelham's battery of horse artillery, left his headquarters at "The Bower" in the Shenandoah Valley and headed into Maryland and Pennsylvania, making his second ride completely around an army commanded by George McClellan (the first had been made during the Peninsula Campaign the previous June). His primary objectives were to learn Union dispositions and intentions for the coming months, and to gather horses to replenish the dwindling stocks of Northern Virginia. After three days and two nights in the saddle, he returned to Virginia by way of White's Ford. He brought with him twelve hundred captured mounts, having left sixty of his own broken-down horses behind. Few of his men remembered the last night's ride after thirty-six hours in the saddle with only a few short breaks; once safely across the river into Virginia, a number of them fell from their horses and slept where they lay. The next morning, they awoke refreshed and joined their comrades near Leesburg.

Stuart and his men had ridden 130 miles in three days, and the last 80 in only twenty-four hours. While most of the command rested in the town for a day, Stuart returned to the Shenandoah Valley, where General Jackson greeted him with as close to a joke as ever passed that stern Presbyterian's lips:

> *They tell me that from the time you crossed the Potomac until you got back you didn't sing or crack a joke, but that as soon as you got on Virginia soil, you began to whistle "Home, Sweet Home."*[54]

THE ARMIES ON THE MOVE

The Army of the Potomac came to Loudoun County for the first time on October 26, 1862, when it began crossing the Potomac on two pontoon bridges at Berlin. Two divisions of infantry and a cavalry brigade crossed first, driving Confederate pickets as far back as Snicker's Gap. Because Lee and the Army of Northern Virginia were still in the Shenandoah Valley, McClellan found himself with the inside track to Richmond, being closer to the Confederate capital than its defenders. To give him time to move up the valley and cross the mountains ahead of the Yankees, Lee ordered Jeb Stuart and his cavalry to slow their advance as much as possible. The order could not have come at a worse time.

Stuart's horses were plagued by a condition known as "grease heel," an infection caused by keeping horses in wet or muddy conditions for extended periods of time. Though it is curable, grease heel can lame a horse. So many of Stuart's cavalry horses were afflicted that he found himself with only a single brigade numbering fewer than a thousand men to impede the progress of the hundred-thousand-man enemy army. The rest of his men were needed to scout ahead of Lee's army and to function as the rear guard as it left the valley and moved south. Stuart's orders were to guard the flanks of Longstreet's infantry, keep the enemy out of the Blue Ridge Mountain gaps and, at the same time, maintain a fifty-mile string of pickets between Longstreet and Jackson. Such an order would have tasked the resources of ten times as many men as Stuart had at his disposal. His only hope was to fight a series of delaying actions along the eastern slope of the mountains to buy time for the slow-moving infantry and their baggage trains.

Even the commander of the single Confederate cavalry brigade operating in the Loudoun Valley was unavailable. Fitzhugh Lee was suffering from one of his frequent illnesses. The next senior officer, W.H.F. "Rooney" Lee, was still recovering from a wound he suffered in the Maryland Campaign. The command then devolved on Colonel Williams C. Wickham of the Fourth Virginia Cavalry. Perhaps it was because of the lack of experienced senior officers that Stuart decided to accompany the brigade and leave close supervision of the rest of the cavalry's tasks to others.

On the evening of the twenty-eighth, John Pelham arrived from Millwood and camped with his battery on Seton Hill, a few miles north of Middleburg. He would move on the next day to join Stuart and Wickham in Bloomfield. He had not been in camp long when a messenger arrived, inviting him and his aide, Lieutenant George Walker, to spend the night at Welbourne, the nearby home of Colonel Richard Dulany of the Seventh Virginia Cavalry. The next morning, Pelham was anxious to return to his battery, but the Dulany family insisted that he stay for breakfast. While the meal was being prepared, Pelham paced nervously in one of the parlors, finally stopping to

Welbourne, the home of Colonel Richard Henry Dulany. *Photo by the author.*

stare out one of the front windows. When young Mary Dulany came in to tell him that breakfast was ready, the major quickly dropped his hand from the window and followed her into the dining room. The family later discovered that he had been using a diamond ring to scratch graffiti into one of the window panes.

GC Walker
Oct 28, 62
J

Since the *J* has the distinctive shape of John Pelham's script, there can be no doubt about who scratched the message into the window. It remains there to this day, a mute witness to the days when armies marched and fought their way across the county.

Stuart "opened the ball" in the Loudoun Valley with an attack on three companies of the First Rhode Island Cavalry at Mountville, where the Snickersville Turnpike crosses Goose Creek. Leaving his Bloomfield bivouac before dawn on October 30, he approached the village by a cart path and surprised the Yankee camp. The charge by the Ninth Virginia Cavalry killed Lieutenant L.D. Gove, the picket commander, and netted fifty prisoners. The rest fled for their lives down the road to Aldie with the Confederates in hot pursuit. As they reached the outskirts of that town, the Confederates found themselves facing the brigade of George D. Bayard, who had come from his camp near Chantilly that morning on a scout toward Ashby's Gap. While Wickham prepared to attack, Pelham's battery traded shots with the Union artillery. Just then, Stuart received word that another large Union force was coming up in his rear from the direction of Leesburg. Moving down the Cobb House Road to the Ashby's Gap Turnpike, he withdrew to a strong defensive position near Middleburg. Bayard, believing that he was facing a superior enemy force, was withdrawing too, leaving eight of his men dead on the field.

The next morning, Stuart moved through Union to meet the enemy as they came south through Philomont. In the heavy woods, most of the Confederate cavalrymen fought dismounted, using the area's many stone walls as breastworks. It would not be the last time the Union cavalry commander, General Alfred Pleasonton, would mistake dismounted cavalry for Confederate infantry; nor would it be the last time he frantically called for infantry support of his own. After spending all day skirmishing, but gaining no ground, Pleasonton got both an infantry brigade, complete with another battery of artillery, and Brigadier General William Averell's cavalry brigade to help him.

With his reinforcements, Pleasonton now had more than twice as many men and cannon as Stuart, and was thus able to drive the Confederates slowly back toward Union. Pelham, posting his guns with great skill, almost single-handedly slowed Pleasonton's advance to a crawl. At one point, he was pressed by a squadron of cavalry that repeatedly rode up to his guns, shot down battery horses and withdrew to nearby woods to reload. Stuart reported what happened next:

It was during this engagement that Major Pelham conducted a howitzer some distance beyond support to a neighboring hill and opened a masked fire upon a body of the enemy's

Major General Alfred Pleasonton.
Courtesy of the Library of Congress.

cavalry in the valley beneath, putting them to flight, capturing their flag and various articles—their arms, equipments, and horses, as well as some prisoners—sustaining in this extraordinary feat no loss whatever.[55]

As superior Union numbers forced Stuart to give up one position after another, the fighting drew inexorably closer to the mountains. Many of Stuart's men were now literally fighting for their homes. Fanny Dulany, the daughter of Colonel Richard Dulany, later recorded Stuart's hurried visit to Welbourne, in the course of that long and trying day:

Gen. Stuart rode up. We asked him if he would not dismount, so as to eat his dinner more comfortably; Thank you ladies said he, but I have not the time. Cousin Julia then handed him a plate with some dinner on it, and then offered him a knife & fork, which however he refused, saying that he was more accustomed to use his fingers, and therefore could eat better with more expedition with them. So Cousin Julia held the plate for him, & he seemed to enjoy his dinner very much. We then filled his knapsack with apples, after which he rode off.[56]

Within the hour, the fighting had reached the yard of Welbourne. "The Yankees came nearer," said Fanny Dulany, "and the bullets ticked on the tin roof like hail. At about five in the evening the whole place was crowded with horrid Yankees."

Stuart fell back past Upperville, where General D.H. Hill asked him to hold Ashby's Gap long enough for Jackson's corps to evacuate the Shenandoah Valley. Stuart made Pleasonton fight all day to gain possession of the town, which still left the Yankees several miles from the vital gap. At this point, he sent the First, Fourth and Fifth Virginia Cavalry, now commanded by Colonel Thomas Rosser, who took over when Wickham was wounded, south toward Piedmont, while he retired to the gap with the Third and Ninth Virginia, expecting soon to be joined by Wade Hampton's brigade. In the gap, Stuart found that Hill had left behind a small infantry force and a twelve-pounder Whitworth gun of Hardaway's Battery that greatly discomfited the Union cavalry by throwing shells all the way from the mountains to Upperville.

The Confederates now abandoned Loudoun County to the tender mercies of hungry Union soldiers. "When morning came," Ida Dulany recorded,

> of our large flock of improved sheep only fifteen could be found, while from one end of the field to the other their skins were dotted about over the ground. They killed several hogs more, every shoat and took most of the cabbage out of the garden.

Stripped of their stored food by the Union army, the citizens of Loudoun were about to enter a long and hungry winter.

Introducing Mosby's Rangers

THE WINTER OF 1862–63

The winter of 1862–63 in Northern Virginia turned out to be an unusually long and hard season of bad weather and above average precipitation. After the slaughter at Fredericksburg in early December, the armies, for the most part, sat quietly along the banks of the Rappahannock River, the Army of Northern Virginia on the south bank and the Army of the Potomac, now commanded by General Ambrose Burnside, on the north. To relieve the boredom of winter camp life and to keep the Yankees from becoming too complacent in their numerical superiority, Jeb Stuart and his cavalry staged a raid behind Burnside's lines, riding through Fairfax County in the vicinity of Washington. Then they moved into Loudoun County for a few days of well-earned rest. Stuart made his temporary headquarters at Oakham Farm, the home of Hamilton Rogers, on the Ashby's Gap Turnpike west of Aldie. While there, he made one of his most momentous decisions of the war, although no one recognized its significance at the time. On the morning of December 31, he gave his permission for John S. Mosby, a scout serving on his staff, to remain in Loudoun County when the rest of the cavalry returned to Fredericksburg. With a detail of nine men borrowed from the First Virginia Cavalry, Mosby was to conduct guerrilla operations along Burnside's line of supply and communications.

A full treatment of the partisan career of Mosby is beyond the scope of this work. Many books have been, and many more will be, written on that subject. This account will focus on the most important of his operations within the borders of Loudoun, and will only touch lightly on what went on in Fairfax, Fauquier and Prince William counties, the other jurisdictions that made up what came to be called "Mosby's Confederacy."

As Mosby and his men watched the last of Stuart's cavalry make their way southward, he instructed the nine men to find lodging in the homes of loyal Southern people, with no more than two men staying in a single place. They were to meet at Mount Zion Church, on the turnpike a couple of miles east of Aldie, ten days later for instructions. Mosby rode only one raid with that original group, a strike at a Union picket post at Herndon Junction on the Alexandria, Loudoun & Hampshire Railroad. They returned with several Union prisoners, their horses and all their military equipment, all of which

Colonel John S. Mosby, photographed in Richmond in 1864. Lying at his feet is the coat worn by General Edwin Stoughton on the night Mosby captured him in Fairfax. *Courtesy of the Stuart-Mosby Historical Society.*

Mount Zion Church was used throughout the war as a hospital by both sides and was the site of an 1864 fight between Mosby's Rangers and the men of the Twenty-second Corps Cavalry Brigade. *Photo by the author.*

they turned over to Stuart at his camp near Fredericksburg. The general was so pleased with the scout's success that he gave him leave to return to Loudoun, this time with fifteen men under his command. Mosby still expected to be ordered to return to Stuart's command in the spring. Neither he nor Stuart realized that this was the beginning of a partisan ranger career that would make Mosby a household name.

THE MISKEL FARM

Mosby spent the week after his return to Northern Virginia scouting the area alone, and this quickly became his preferred way of preparing for a raid. On January 28, he met his men at Mount Zion Church. With him was his first new recruit, John Underwood of Fairfax, who "knew the county better than the wild animals that roamed over it by night or by day."[57]

Near Chantilly, the group surprised a Federal cavalry outpost and rode away into the night with nine prisoners, their horses and equipment. When he heard of the attack, Colonel Percy Wyndham of the First New Jersey Cavalry ordered two hundred men in pursuit to Middleburg. Mosby and Fount Beattie were asleep in the Lorman Chancellor home when a servant ran in to warn them of the Yankees' approach. Rising and dressing quickly, the men mounted their horses and, with six other men, they charged the rear of the Union column as it left the town. In the ensuing mêlée, one Yankee was killed and three captured, but Mosby also had three men captured—the first men lost under his command. Still, the sudden attack, the futile Union pursuit and Mosby's counterattack set a pattern that would become all too familiar to frustrated Federal officers over the course of the next two years.

Throughout the month of February, Mosby made a number of raids against Union outposts and pickets while familiarizing himself with the area. He and his growing band wrote their names into the history books on the night of March 8 when they rode boldly into the heart of the Union camp at Fairfax and rode out with General Edwin Stoughton, his staff and more than fifty fine horses. The ensuing shakeup of the Union forces in Northern Virginia diverted more than a brigade's worth of men from the front lines and put them to work either pursuing Mosby or guarding supply depots and important communications hubs far to the rear of the Army of the Potomac's Rappahannock River position, the very effect Mosby most wanted to achieve.

By the end of March, newly promoted Captain Mosby had been joined by nearly fifty additional men. He rode into Fairfax County on March 31 with sixty men—his largest strike force to date—hoping to "flush something out," only to find that his earlier raids had caused the Yankees to pull their advance pickets back to the east of Difficult Run to get them within supporting distance of their main camps. Frustrated, tired and cold, Mosby and his band rode to the farm of Thomas and Lydia Miskel on the banks of the Potomac River to seek food and shelter for themselves and forage for their horses. Mosby and a few others went to sleep on the floor of the house while most of the men and the horses bedded down in the Miskel's spacious barn.

Their passage through Western Fairfax and Eastern Loudoun Counties did not go unnoticed. An anonymous Union sympathizer rode into Major Charles F. Taggart's camp at Union Church and informed him of Mosby's presence in Eastern Loudoun. Taggart quickly summoned Captain Henry C. Flint and instructed him to take 150 men of the First Vermont Cavalry to capture or kill the Rebel raiders. The detachment left camp at 2:00 a.m. and headed for Dranesville, where they had been told Mosby would be spending the night. As they approached the village, Flint divided his force, keeping half with him and sending the others with Captain George H. Bean to surround the place and prevent the escape of their quarry. They had not searched many houses before they learned that Mosby and his band had passed through Dranesville on their way to the Miskel Farm the night before but had not stopped.

Since it had snowed the day before, Mosby's trail was not hard to follow. Lieutenant Josiah Grout later reported that the Vermonters followed it westward along the Leesburg Pike (modern Route 7) until it turned north on the road leading to the Miskel Farm (now Broad Run Drive), "a poor, muddy road that led through a dwarf growth of timber."[58] Around daylight, Flint stopped briefly at a home on the pike, possibly to make sure there was not another route Mosby could have used to leave the farm without retracing his steps. Their stopping was a lucky break for Mosby. One of his men, a forty-nine-year-old Methodist preacher named Dick Moran, had spent the night in the house, and he hid beneath the stairs while Flint talked with the inhabitants. As the Vermonters moved on, Captain Flint gleefully cried, "All right boys; now we'll give Mosby an April Fool!" Moran rushed out behind them to saddle his horse for a two-mile race across the countryside to the Miskel Farm.

Mosby, knowing the nearest Union camp was nine miles away, had not placed guards on the road. Only a single sentry stood watch over the horses penned in the Miskel barnyard. "My authority over the men was of such transitory nature that I disliked to order them to do anything but fight," Mosby later explained.[59] That omission could have cost him dearly.

If Flint had designed a trap for Mosby and his men, he could not have come up with a better one than the Miskel Farm. The Potomac River was only a few hundred yards to the north of the home, with Broad Run to the west and heavy timber on the east and south of the cleared farmland. The only road offering access to the property was not only filled with blue-clad troopers, but it was also lined on both sides by a high plank fence with heavy gates at both the entrance to the farm and the barnyard where most of Mosby's men still lay sleeping with their horses unsaddled.

Just as the Union cavalry exited the woods and came to the cleared fields of the farm, a galloping horse and rider burst from the trees to their right and cut into the road in front of them. It was Dick Moran, frantically waving his hat and hollering at the top of his preacher lungs, "Mount your horses! The Yankees are coming!"

Mosby, always an early riser, had just walked out onto the porch of the farmhouse when he heard Moran's shout. He immediately ran down the hill to the barnyard, adding his own shouted warning to Moran's cries. Confederate soldiers began to pour from the barn, some only half dressed, and they frantically checked their weapons and saddled their horses. By the time Mosby reached the fence surrounding the barnyard, the place was "alive with excitement," in the words of one guerrilla. The shots and shouts of Flint's men mingled with Rebel yells and the screams of wounded horses in what must have been an incredible din.

Here Captain Flint made a fatal mistake. As the last Union cavalryman passed through the gate between the farm lane and the fenced road to the barn, Flint had them close and barricade the gate to prevent the escape of any Rebels lucky enough to break through the Vermonters' line. He then divided his force, sending Captain Bean and fifty men around the fence line to the left to prevent the escape of any men who might try to make their way to the river. Had Flint had his carbine-armed men surround the farm just beyond Mosby's revolver range (about thirty yards), they could have picked off the Confederates one by one or forced them to run a gauntlet of fire in an attempt to escape. Instead, he ordered a saber charge down the narrow roadway toward a second gate near the barn.

"Captain Flint believed in cold steel for the rebels," wrote Lieutenant Grout.

> *It was his notion that they would not stand in a fight where the saber was foremost, so his orders were to use freely the blades we had so carefully sharpened about a year before.*

Caleb Rector home in Rector's Crossroads (Atoka). Here Mosby formed Company A of his Forty-third Virginia Partisan Rangers. *Photo by the author.*

Mosby and his men, however, were doing more than standing before Flint's saber charge. They had reacted so quickly to Moran's warning that Grout described them as drawn up in line "in full readiness to receive us" by the time the end of the Federal column emerged from the woods. For several minutes, as Flint prepared his saber charge, the two forces exchanged fire, the Yankees with their single-shot carbines and the Confederates with their six-shooters. At least two of the Union soldiers were killed in an attempt to either open the second gate or break down the fence to allow entrance to the barnyard. Finally, the gate was opened, and Flint cried to his men, "Come on! Get at them with the saber!" According to Confederate accounts, Flint burst through the gate swinging his saber and shouting, "Kill all the damned cowards!" Whatever he shouted, he immediately fell dead with six bullets in his body.

Seeing Flint fall and suddenly realizing they were trapped between a wall of revolver fire and the high fence along the lane, the Vermonters first faltered in their attack and then began to panic. Mosby, still on foot, held open the barnyard gate and loudly called to his men, "Follow me! Charge them! Charge them, and go right through them!" Few men have ever led a cavalry charge on foot, but Mosby, seizing on the enemy's confusion, turned instantly from prey to predator and was too anxious to get at them to wait for his horse.

At the barnyard gate, now held open by John Farrar, Harry Hatcher handed Mosby the reins of a saddled horse. The captain quickly mounted and led approximately twenty other mounted men in a furious assault on the frightened Yankees, whose escape was blocked by fallen horses and men and by the barricaded gate at the far end of the lane. The fight in the lane was brief, with the Yankees soon fleeing "in fearful confusion," closely pursued by Mosby and his mounted men.

The first of the Union cavalrymen to break through the barricaded gate was Captain Bean. Before he even reached his assigned position, he heard the firing and saw Captain Flint fall from his horse. At that, he abandoned his men and raced to save himself. Mounted on a good horse, he was the first of the survivors to return to their Union Church camp. Within a month of the Miskel Farm fight, he would be dismissed from the service for cowardice.

Mosby and his men pursued the Vermont cavalrymen for nearly six miles after another brief fight at the intersection of the farm road and the Turnpike, where Lieutenant C.A. Woodbury died trying to rally the survivors. When it was all over, Mosby reported nine Union soldiers killed, fifteen wounded and eighty-two captured. With them, he took more than ninety horses with all their equipment and more than a hundred sabers, carbines and revolvers. He left the wounded too seriously hurt to move, including Lieutenant Grout, in the Miskel home, but took three others to a hospital in Middleburg.

Mosby's own losses were four wounded—Ned Hurst, William Keyes, R.A. Hart and a man named Davis from Kentucky. The latter died of his wounds in the Miskel living room the next morning. He was the first man to lose his life serving under Mosby's command.

In the grand scheme of the war, the fight at the Miskel Farm meant little, but Captain Flint would not be the last Union officer to learn the fearful advantages of Mosby's style of fighting at arm's length with a revolver in each hand over Union sabers and carbines;

A fanciful artist's conception of the fight at the Miskel Farm between Mosby's Rangers and the First Vermont Cavalry. *Courtesy of the Library of Congress.*

nor would he be the last to learn that Mosby, when caught at a disadvantage, was much more likely to strike back than to run. Among all his other skills, Mosby was incredibly lucky. "Never before or after," wrote Ranger John Munson, "had the federal troops such another chance to secure Mosby and wipe out his men."[60] Over the next two years, many a Union officer would rue Flint's failure.

Prelude to Gettysburg

Because the winter was unusually long and hard all over Virginia, the 1863 military campaign season was late getting started. On May 1, the Army of Northern Virginia and the Army of the Potomac, which was now commanded by General Joseph Hooker, were engaged in a brutal struggle at an obscure wilderness crossroads called Chancellorsville. The battle was a resounding Confederate victory, but it was won at a terrible price. The great Stonewall Jackson lay numbered among the dead.

For a month after the fighting at Chancellorsville, the two armies sat facing each other across the Rappahannock River near Fredericksburg. During the first week of June, however, Lee's army slipped out of its camps along the river and simply disappeared into the heavily wooded area known as the Wilderness. Hooker knew only that they were gone; knowledge he confirmed by tentative probes across the river. By June 9, when his cavalry clashed with Stuart's horsemen at Brandy Station in the largest cavalry battle ever fought on the North American continent, he knew Lee was heading west. Lee's ultimate objective, though, was anyone's guess.

Rumors abounded that Lee was trying to repeat the sort of grand flanking move that had brought John Pope's Army of Virginia to disaster at Second Manassas nine months earlier. Other rumors said he was planning to double back and race around Hooker's flank to get between the Army of the Potomac and Washington.

Meanwhile, certain the Rebels were headed in his direction, Governor Andrew Curtin of Pennsylvania bombarded Washington with demands for troops, arms and military supplies. Slowly and cautiously, Hooker began to move his divisions northward to keep his men between the Blue Ridge Mountains and Washington. By June 13, Hooker knew a sizeable portion of Lee's army was in the Shenandoah Valley attacking the Union garrisons in Winchester and Berryville. Two days later, on the same day Winchester fell to the Confederates, Hooker established his headquarters in Fairfax, where he would remain for more than a week.

Hooker positioned his troops well, covering all possible approaches to the capital. The I Corps camped at Guilford Station (present-day Sterling) on the Alexandria, Loudoun & Hampshire Railroad (now the Washington & Old Dominion Bike Trail), with the

III Corps in Gum Springs and the V Corps in Aldie. The II Corps was at Sangster's Station (soon to move to Thoroughfare Gap), the XII Corps in Leesburg, the VI Corps in Germantown and the XI Corps at Trappe Rock on Goose Creek. Should Lee show himself from either the west or the south, the army could be reunited quickly to oppose him. To offer serious resistance to Lee's plans, however, Hooker had to know whether the Confederates who were entering Maryland and Pennsylvania were a mere raiding party or the vanguard of an invading army. The only way to know that was to find Lee as quickly as possible.

Hooker ordered his cavalry to move west through the Loudoun Valley and cross the Blue Ridge into the Shenandoah, regardless of the cost. "It is better that we should lose men," he wrote to cavalry commander Alfred Pleasonton, "than to be without knowledge of the enemy."[61] The Union cavalry's first objective was the village of Aldie and the vital intersection of the Ashby's Gap and Snickersville Turnpikes. Unless he could control these highways, there would be no way for him to reach the Shenandoah and carry out Hooker's orders.

ALDIE

Judson Kilpatrick's brigade of Union cavalry reached Aldie around two thirty on the afternoon of June 17 to be met by pickets from the Sixth Virginia Cavalry who had been ordered to guard the intersection of the Little River Turnpike and the Carolina Road (modern Routes 50 and 15, which intersect at Gilbert's Corner). The brief exchange of gunfire was a shock because Stuart was believed to be west of the Blue Ridge; nevertheless, Kilpatrick quickly ordered two companies of the Second New York Cavalry to attack and drive the enemy through the town. As the New Yorkers galloped through the village, they were met by Colonel Thomas Rosser and the Fifth Virginia Cavalry coming from the other direction. After a short, but nasty, saber fight, both sides withdrew to assess the situation. Neither had expected to fight in Aldie.

Colonel Munford, once again commanding the brigade in Fitz Lee's absence, positioned his men astride both turnpikes, the First, Fourth and Fifth Virginia and James Breathed's artillery battery on a ridge blocking the Ashby's Gap road and the Second and Third Virginia to the north guarding the road to Snicker's Gap. Munford went with the latter, leaving Colonel Wickham in command of the troops on the right flank. The first phase of the battle began to play out when Rosser posted Captain Reuben Boston and approximately fifty men of the Fifth Virginia along a ridge some six hundred yards in front of the main Confederate line. They immediately came under fire from the guns of Captain Alanson Randol's combined Batteries E and G, First U.S. Artillery (the same guns that would open the Battle of Gettysburg two weeks later). For a short time, they were answered by two of Breathed's guns posted in an orchard behind Boston's position, but the Confederate guns soon pulled back to the more distant main position.

Boston was then attacked by the Second New York Cavalry, but he easily repulsed them, inflicting heavy losses. Kilpatrick, who would commit his forces to the fight piecemeal all day, then sent the Sixth Ohio to their assistance. After a bloody fight, the two regiments forced Boston's small detachment to surrender. It was the first time a company-size body of Stuart's troops had ever surrendered on the battlefield. Boston would spend nine months as a prisoner of war, only to face a court-martial when he returned. The court, however, would find him innocent and rule that the blame for his surrender was Rosser's for placing the men too far forward to be adequately supported by the rest of the regiment.

Boston's surrender ended the fight along the Ashby's Gap Turnpike. The action now shifted to the north, where dismounted Confederate sharpshooters who were posted behind stone walls awaited an attack by the First Massachusetts Cavalry. At about the same time that the New Yorkers first attacked Boston, Major Henry Higginson led a squadron (two companies) of the Bay Staters north on the Snickersville Pike. For the next three hours, the fighting along the road would seesaw back and forth as the First Massachusetts, later supported by the Fourth New York and the First Maine, traded shots and saber blows with the Second, Third, Fourth and Fifth Virginia and one of Breathed's cannon. Attacking down a narrow road bordered on both sides by high stone walls, one Union squadron after another galloped around a blind curve only to find the road filled with dead and wounded men and horses. By the time it was over, the First Massachusetts had suffered more than two hundred casualties, the severest losses experienced by any Union cavalry regiment on a single day in the entire war.

Munford always considered Aldie to be a Confederate victory, but as darkness began to fall that night, he withdrew from the field in obedience to an order from Stuart, who had problems of his own in Middleburg.

MIDDLEBURG

Stuart had accompanied Munford as far as Middleburg on the morning march, but he had decided to stop there since it was a more central location from which to keep in touch with his scattered brigades. In addition to sending Munford to Aldie, he had sent Colonel John Chambliss, who was temporarily commanding Rooney Lee's brigade, south to watch Thoroughfare Gap, while he ordered General Beverly Robertson and his brigade of green North Carolina troopers to reconnoiter toward Rectortown in Fauquier County before rejoining the rest of the cavalry in Middleburg.

At three o'clock that morning, as the Union cavalry began their march to Aldie, Pleasonton and Kilpatrick had detached the First Rhode Island Cavalry from the rest of the brigade and sent it by itself to scout Thoroughfare Gap before moving on to camp for the night in Middleburg. The commander of the First Rhode Island, Colonel Alfred Duffié, was out of favor at headquarters. He was a foreigner; a Frenchman who had served in Algiers and the Crimea before moving to America. In addition, he had performed poorly as a division commander at Brandy Station. Pleasonton, who later said, "I have no faith in foreigners saving our Government or country,"[62] reorganized the Cavalry Corps after that battle, putting David McM. Gregg in command of the division and relegating Duffié to regimental command once again. Whether the First Rhode

Island was sent off on its own to punish its commanding officer or simply to get them out of sight and out of mind, it would turn out to be a tragic mistake.

When Duffié's men reached Thoroughfare Gap, they encountered pickets of the Ninth Virginia Cavalry under Colonel Richard Beale. Because he had been ordered not to engage the enemy, Beale simply stepped aside and let the Rhode Islanders continue on the road to Middleburg. Knowing now that a brigade of Confederate cavalry was behind him, Duffié soon got the unwelcome news that Stuart and another brigade were in front near Middleburg.

When the Yankees rode into town, Stuart and his staff were eating lunch. With no more protection than his staff, a few couriers and a company of Fourth Virginia troopers, Stuart was forced to beat a hasty retreat. Theodore Garnett, one of his aides, later described how "with no little mortification, General Stuart turned his horse's head toward Upperville."[63] They had not gone far before they encountered Robertson's Carolinians, approaching from Rector's Crossroads (now called Atoka). Duffié, in the meantime, had ordered his men to barricade the roads into town. Despite knowing that he was threatened by at least two brigades of enemy cavalry, he was determined to obey his orders to stay the night in Middleburg.

As darkness fell, Major Heros von Borcke, one of Stuart's aides, led the Carolinians in a charge into the town and then down The Plains Road, where Duffié had fallen back to make camp. In the darkness, ambushed by Union cavalrymen behind the stone walls on both sides of the road and entangled in the branches of felled trees, the Carolinians suffered terribly; but they soon began to capture Yankees by the dozen. The next morning, Duffié awoke to find himself surrounded. His regiment quickly broke down, with every man trying to escape the trap on his own. By the time the last stragglers made it back to Union lines, their losses totaled 6 dead, 9 wounded and 210 captured out of the 300 or so who had ridden off on this fool's errand a day earlier.

OPEN SESAME

Around 10:00 p.m. on June 17, John Mosby and a small band of his men captured two Union officers near Aldie. They turned out to be couriers carrying dispatches from the army command to the troops in the Loudoun Valley. Mosby later said that the documents they carried were the "open sesame to all of Hooker's plans and secrets."[64] Along with the strength and dispositions of the entire Union army, the papers revealed that George Meade's V Corps had been ordered to Aldie to support Pleasonton in his attempt to reach the mountains. This convinced Stuart that his plan of action for the coming days would have to be purely defensive; a fighting withdrawal to the mountains to buy as much time as possible to hide the northward move of Lee's army in the Shenandoah. It was not Stuart's preferred way to fight, but it was the best way to carry out his orders to screen the army's advance.

MOUNT DEFIANCE

Just west of Middleburg on the turnpike (Route 50) is a small hill known as Mount Defiance. It was here that Stuart decided to set up his defenses to avoid having to fight inside the village itself. On June 18, John Irvin Gregg, the cousin of division commander David Gregg, brought his brigade to town, accompanied by Battery C, Third U.S. Artillery. Gregg's men saw, but did not seriously press, the Confederate brigade posted along the crest of Mount Defiance. Instead, Union and Confederate artillery engaged in a protracted long-range duel until early evening, when the Yankees withdrew to camp about a mile and a half east of town. In two days, Pleasonton had advanced less than six miles toward his objective. The brigade he sent toward Snicker's Gap fared no better. After approaching to within three miles of the gap, they returned to Aldie without a fight.

On the morning of June 19, the Union cavalry returned to Middleburg to find Stuart in a strong position with two brigades and two batteries of artillery blocking the way. They would now have a hard fight to take a position that might have been had for the asking the day before. For several hours, the fighting consisted only of artillery fire and an occasional shot from the dismounted skirmishers on both sides. Around 10:00 a.m., however, General David Gregg ordered his cousin to attack as soon as he was reinforced by three additional regiments. The fighting was hard and bloody, much of it done "Indian style," with dismounted men dodging from tree to tree in the woods on the south side of the turnpike. Eventually, superior Union numbers forced Stuart to pull his brigades back to the next ridgeline west of town.

While doing this, he suffered a serious loss when Major von Borcke received a dangerous bullet wound in his throat. Told that the wound was mortal, Stuart sent von Borcke to Upperville to the home of Dr. Talcott Eliason, the Cavalry Corps surgeon. To Eliason's surprise, von Borcke did not die, although he was unable to return to active duty in the Confederate army.

To the north, John Buford's brigades had skirmished with Confederate pickets at a crossroads village known as Pothouse (now Leithtown). As he slowly moved westward along the north bank of Goose Creek, Buford received orders to detach his Reserve Brigade, the First, Second, Fifth and Sixth U.S. Cavalry, to reinforce Gregg in Middleburg. It was these troops coming in on his left flank that forced Stuart to abandon the Mount Defiance line.

The fighting on Mount Defiance petered out by early afternoon. Pleasonton was apparently satisfied with having driven Stuart back from his first defensive position. While General Hooker grew increasingly frustrated with the lack of hard information about Lee's location and intentions, Pleasonton once again surrendered his hard-won advantage. He had lost men, but he was no closer to knowledge of the enemy's plan than he had been two days earlier when the fighting started at Aldie.

WEST TO UPPERVILLE

Both sides received reinforcements during the night of June 19–20. Stuart would begin the next day's actions with the brigades of Wade Hampton and William E. "Grumble" Jones in addition to those of the two Lees and Beverly Robertson. With extra manpower available, he extended his screening line to the north, sending Munford (Fitz Lee's brigade) to Snickersville and Jones and Chambliss (Rooney Lee's brigade) to Union, while keeping Hampton and Robertson on the line west of Middleburg. On the other side of the field, Pleasonton finally got the infantry support he had requested. Strong Vincent's brigade from the First Division of George Meade's V Corps, a brigade that would win fame on the slopes of Little Round Top two weeks later in Gettysburg, marched out of Aldie before dawn to join the cavalry in Middleburg.

Had June 21 not been a Sunday, Stuart might have launched the first attack of the day. He decided, however, "to do no duty other than what was absolutely necessary, and determined, so far as was in my power, to devote [the day] to rest."[65] Pleasonton had other ideas. The action started at 8:00 a.m. with an hour-long artillery duel, and progressed to a combined cavalry-infantry attack on the Confederate position. Four regiments of Union infantry soon outflanked Stuart's right, and he issued orders to begin withdrawing to another line west of Goose Creek. About the time the last two guns of James Hart's battery of horse artillery began to limber up, an artillery shell hit and exploded the ammunition chest of one of them, killing or wounding every horse and driver of its team. Before a replacement team could be brought up, the gun was overrun and captured by Union infantrymen—the first of Stuart's cannon ever to be captured in battle.

Stuart next made a stand at the stone bridge over which the turnpike crossed Goose Creek. His dismounted sharpshooters and artillery were able to repulse several Union attempts to cross the bridge before the infantry slid down the steep bank, waded across the shallow creek and drove the Confederates back. Although he had gained several hours more time, Stuart now had to fall all the way back to Upperville, only a few miles from Ashby's Gap. Meanwhile, a couple of miles to the north, Jones and Chambliss were

A contemporary illustration of the fighting in Upperville on June 21, 1863. *Courtesy of* Harper's Weekly.

slowly withdrawing along a parallel road, stopping frequently to delay Buford's attempts to reach the mountains or to reinforce Gregg's fight along the turnpike.

Although Stuart did not want to fight in Upperville any more than he had wanted to fight in Middleburg, Gregg left him little choice. His first defensive position was on the east side of the village, with Robertson in the Ivy Hill Cemetery on the north side of the highway and Hampton on the south side on a broad ridge known as Vineyard Hill. Just as Kilpatrick's depleted brigade began to charge up the hill, the Carolinians looked to their left and saw Buford's brigade charging in their direction a little more than a mile away. Not seeing Jones and Chambliss between their position and Buford's, Robertson's men broke and fled through town before Kilpatrick even reached them. Hampton, however, struck the pursuing Yankees on their flank and drove them back. In a confusing battle of charge and countercharge, Hampton was able to halt the advance of two Union brigades with only three of his regiments. John Esten Cooke, a member of Stuart's staff, later wrote of the general's personal involvement in the Upperville fighting:

> *Here in the edge of the town a fierce hand to hand fight took place and Stuart fought with the men like a common soldier. I have never witnessed a greater "jumble" of gray and blue.*[66]

At the same time Hampton and Gregg were fighting in Upperville, Buford had finally brought Jones and Chambliss to bay as they crossed the farm of George Ayre and approached Trappe Road. William Gamble's brigade, using a hidden farm lane known as the Sunken Road, hit Chambliss in the flank. Only the well-served guns of Preston Chew's battery of horse artillery prevented a Confederate disaster. As the fighting went on in a broad field between Ayreshire and Kirkby, the home of the Thomas family, Buford's charging regiments were seen by the Carolinians in Upperville, precipitating their flight through the village. Robertson's retreat left the road to Upperville and Ashby's Gap blocked, and threatened to cut off Jones and Chambliss from the rest of Stuart's cavalry. Fortunately, Captain Bruce Gibson of the Sixth Virginia Cavalry was a local boy who showed Jones a back road to the mountains and enabled the brigades to make their escape. As the sun set on the battlefield, Gregg made one more effort to follow Stuart into the gap, but he was handily repulsed by the rallied North Carolinians. As darkness fell, he pulled back and went into camp in the fields of Upperville.

The next morning, Stuart and his men woke to find the Union cavalry withdrawing toward Aldie once again. Pleasonton proudly assured General Hooker that there were no Confederate infantry in the Loudoun Valley, conveniently overlooking the fact that he still could not tell the army commander where the Confederate infantry were. The battles were over for the time being, but the blue and gray cavalries would continue to skirmish for the next two days until Pleasonton quit the valley.

In the end, it was not Hooker's cavalry, but his signal officers, who gave him the information he needed on the whereabouts and intentions of the Army of Northern Virginia. On June 24, word came from the signal station on Maryland Heights, overlooking Harpers Ferry, that "large trains are crossing [the Potomac] at Sharpsburg. Artillery and general trains are passing near Charlestown toward Shepherdstown."[67]

Obviously, Lee had begun his second invasion of the North.

Now certain that the Confederates were not planning to fall upon Washington, Hooker sent his final orders through the telegraph/signal flag network at Guilford Station, setting his scattered divisions and corps in motion for a rendezvous at Edwards Ferry near Leesburg. There, they left Virginia by way of two newly built pontoon bridges and entered Maryland, heading toward a climactic meeting at Gettysburg. By the time the armies met there, George Meade, a native of Pennsylvania, had replaced Hooker as commander of the Army of the Potomac.

Portions of both armies passed through Loudoun County on the way back to the Rappahannock at the conclusion of the Gettysburg Campaign, but for all intents, Loudoun had seen its last battle. The killing would continue in the county in smaller skirmishes and raids as Mosby, gaining experience and recruits, made life "behind the lines" a hazardous proposition for any man wearing the Union blue.

Mosby's Confederacy

By January 1864, only one Union officer, Major Henry Cole, had managed to achieve any sort of consistent success in combating John Mosby's Partisan Rangers. Using Mosby's own hit-and-run tactics against him, Cole and his First Maryland Potomac Home Brigade operated out of the unionist northern portion of Loudoun to stage surprise raids on Leesburg, Middleburg and other Mosby strongholds. At the same time, cavalry patrols from the defenses of Washington frequently passed through Loudoun's towns and villages searching for the partisans and their plunder.

LOUDOUN HEIGHTS

Cole and his men were in winter quarters on the Loudoun Heights, guarding the southern and eastern approaches to Harpers Ferry, when Major Frank Stringfellow of Jeb Stuart's staff came to Mosby with a proposition that his small band of scouts should join forces with Mosby's larger command to capture Cole in his camp. Mosby agreed, and on the night of January 10 he left Upperville with 106 men to rendezvous with Stringfellow near Hillsboro. It was a miserably cold night, with more than a foot of snow on the ground. The plan was for Mosby and his men to sneak up on the camp while Stringfellow and his 10 men slipped around it to capture Cole in the house he used as his headquarters. Unfortunately, before Mosby's men were in position, someone fired a shot, instantly waking the Union soldiers. In the ensuing confusion, Mosby's and Stringfellow's men fired on each other, killing and wounding a number of their own men.

From a strong defensive position inside a log building, Cole's men poured deadly carbine and revolver fire into the confused Confederate ranks. By the time Mosby managed to get his men under control and break off the engagement, he left five men dead on the field and took away three others who were mortally wounded and nearly a dozen men with less serious wounds. He left behind one man who was taken prisoner. In exchange, he captured six of Cole's men and approximately fifty horses. It was one of the worst defeats of Mosby's entire career. Ranger James Williamson wrote in his memoirs that

> *Even* [Major Mosby], *though he usually appeared cold and unyielding, could not conceal his disappointment and keen regret at the result of this enterprise. He knew and felt that he had suffered a loss which could not well be repaired.*[68]

THE MEN FROM CALIFORNIA

Mosby was not one to stay discouraged for long. Not even the loss of three promising officers could deter him from his mission to make life miserable for the enemy far behind the front lines of the war. In his career as a Partisan, Mosby crossed the paths of many Union cavalrymen, but none got to know him any better than the men of the California Battalion (Companies A, E, F, L and M, Second Massachusetts Cavalry). The Battalion was unique because it was the only organized body of troops serving in the East that had actually been recruited in California (unlike two infantry regiments, the Seventy-first Pennsylvania and the Thirty-second New York, who both called themselves the "First California" because the leaders of both regiments had lived for long periods of time in California). Colonel Charles Russell Lowell, the Boston Brahmin who commanded the new regiment, tried hard to get his command attached to the Army of the Potomac, but the War Department decided they were more valuable in the defenses of Washington. Working mostly with the Thirteenth and Sixteenth New York Cavalries, the Second Massachusetts spent much of 1863 patrolling Northern Virginia and Western Maryland in a vain attempt to curb the increasing "depredations" of Mosby and his men. This mission brought them frequently to Loudoun County.

The Californians first visited Virginia by way of White's Ford on June 17, 1863. Like many of their missions, it was a futile attempt to catch Mosby after he attacked the camp of the Sixth Michigan Cavalry near Edwards's Ferry. Lowell's command on that inaugural raid consisted of six companies of the Second Massachusetts and three of "Scott's 900" (Eleventh New York Cavalry). They rode from their camp near Washington to Leesburg and down the Carolina Road to find Aldie filled with Pleasonton's troopers, who had just begun the Loudoun Valley campaign. The next day, men from Massachusetts and New York returned to camp after a ride of 150 miles, "having accomplished nothing but tiring out both men and horses."[69] It was to be a common pattern of Union responses to Mosby's activities.

ANKER'S SHOP

On February 22, 1864, Mosby knew that Major J. Sewell Reed had come to Loudoun on a scouting expedition with a detachment of approximately 150 men of the Second Massachusetts and Sixteenth New York. They were led by a man named Charles Binns, a Loudoun County native, whose grandfather and great-grandfather had held the office

Colonel Charles Russell Lowell, Second Massachusetts Cavalry. *Courtesy of Larry Rogers.*

of clerk of the Loudoun County Court for eighty years between them. Binns had ridden for a time with Mosby, but after killing another ranger in a drunken brawl, he had deserted and offered his services to the Union cavalry as a scout. The first raid he led for Lowell netted nearly 30 of Mosby's men and a number of fine horses. In the wake of that success, he became one of Colonel Lowell's favorite scouts.

Major Reed had learned the lessons of the previous eight months well. No longer did the Union cavalry count on superior numbers alone to give them victory in fights with Mosby's men. When they marched, they were prepared for action at a moment's notice. Three videttes (mounted pickets) rode in front, followed by twenty-five more two hundred yards behind them and then the main body two hundred yards farther back. The men in the front, supported by the nearest twenty-five men, would give warning of trouble in the road ahead, allowing time for the main body to prepare for action before the guerrillas struck them.[70]

To combat this formation, Mosby placed fifteen dismounted men in a heavy pine wood on the south side of the Leesburg Pike near the Anker blacksmith shop (the vicinity of present-day Sterling). To the east of them, he posted a company led by Lieutenant Frank Williams to charge Reed's men from the front, while another company led by Captain William Chapman hid in the trees some distance to the west to take the Yankees in the rear. Lieutenant Frank Rahm and two other men were instructed to ride out into the road in front of the enemy, engage their videttes in conversation and give the main body time to bunch up before a blast from Mosby's whistle signaled the attack.

Mosby chose his ambush site carefully. With thick timber on the south side of the pike and fences on the north side, Reed's men had nowhere to go but up or down the narrow highway. Mosby's plan could have worked even better than it did had he not blown his whistle too soon and launched the attack not on the main body of Union troops, but on the advance party. Ranger John Munson described the situation:

> When Chapman charged upon the pike, he was abreast of the main body which had turned and begun retreating. When Mosby appeared on the pike…none of the enemy were in front of him and we had to gallop up the pike to catch up with them.[71]

For a time, Reed's men gave a good account of themselves in the hand-to-hand mêlée. The Californians, who Munson called "notoriously good fighters," stood "up to the rack like men, dealing out…the best they had. They rallied at every call on them and went down with banners flying." Reed, whose horse had fallen, was on foot when he seriously wounded one of Mosby's men and was, in return, immediately shot in the face and killed. Captain George Manning went down when his horse fell on his leg and pinned him to the ground. At this point, the Californians managed to open gaps in the fences and they began to flee toward the Potomac River to the north. Many were chased down and captured, some are said to have drowned in the river and others managed to make their escape through the thick timber.

When the smoke cleared, Mosby had suffered one man killed, four seriously wounded and several men with minor wounds. The Californians left eight dead and twenty-five wounded, some of whom were among the seventy-two prisoners Mosby reported. Ninety horses and their equipment also fell into his hands. By the time Colonel Lowell arrived with a relief party the next morning, the prisoners and their captors were long gone, and he had to be content with gathering up the dead and returning them to camp for burial.

MOUNT ZION CHURCH

There would not be another fight of the magnitude of the Anker's Shop affair in Loudoun until July 1864. Mosby and his men decided to celebrate the Fourth of July by raiding the community of Point of Rocks, Maryland. It would come to be known as the "Calico Raid" because so many of the men came back heavily laden with bolts of cloth they had taken from the town's stores. When they returned, Mosby was told that Major William Forbes and between 100 and 150 Second Massachusetts and Thirteenth New York cavalrymen were in Leesburg looking for him. Ranger John Alexander's assessment of the situation was that Forbes was "looking with the same ardor with which the boy sought work—praying that he might not find it."[72] By the time Mosby and his men reached Leesburg the next morning, spoiling for a fight, Forbes had left, heading south toward Aldie and away from the area Mosby had raided the day before.

Taking a back road out of town, Mosby planned to reach Ball's Mill, where the road to Mount Zion Church crossed Goose Creek, to prepare an ambush similar to the one that had worked so well for him at Anker's Shop. Not long after arriving, however, he realized that Forbes had taken a different road south. Moving by yet another "obscure road," he still managed to put his command in a position between the Californians and their camp in Vienna. Mosby found Forbes and his men having lunch and feeding their horses at the home of Samuel Skinner, just to the east of Mount Zion Church on the Little River Turnpike. Forbes had half his men dismount, tend to their horses and eat while the other half remained mounted and ready for action. When they finished, they remounted and gave the other half a chance to relax. In addition, he posted pickets about half a mile away to both the east and the west to alert him to an enemy's approach.

When Mosby arrived, he had with him a small cannon that he placed in the road about a mile to the east of Forbes's position. He ordered Lieutenant Harry Hatcher and a dozen men to go first, while the remainder of the 160 rangers waited for Mosby's signal to advance. Hatcher's party quickly drove the Union pickets back to their main body, which was forming up in two lines in the field east of the Skinner home. As Hatcher galloped up the pike and dismounted several men to start taking down the fence along the road, Mosby ordered his gun crew to fire. The shell exploded in the air far behind the waiting Yankees, but its noise was enough to frighten some of their poorly trained horses and throw their defensive formation into confusion. Before Forbes could re-form his lines, Mosby's men galloped through the fence and slammed into them with wild yells and blazing revolvers.

"At first," wrote Ranger John Munson, "Forbes [sic] men made a good fight, but they could not stand the rain of our pistol balls. We split their front rank asunder and broke their spirit."[73] Nathan Huestis of the Second Massachusetts later wrote, "We fought with desperation for we knew it was death or Richmond with us, but we could not stand it long."[74] The Yankees who were not already dead or wounded retreated to a line of trees near the church and rallied around Major Forbes to make another stand. This position, too, was overrun, and Forbes himself was taken out of action and captured when his horse was shot and fell on him, pinning him to the ground. The action then took on the appearance of a fox hunt, with Mosby's men scattering to chase fleeing Union cavalrymen as far as Sudley Church, a full ten miles from the battlefield. When darkness finally put an end to the pursuit, the rangers had killed twelve, wounded thirty-seven and captured forty-five of the men in blue.[75] Mosby had seven men wounded, one of whom would die the next day, and he brought away more than a hundred Union horses and their equipment.[76]

After this fight, Mosby's war moved away from Loudoun County for the most part as he spent a good deal of time in Maryland and the Shenandoah Valley in support of Jubal Early's raid on Washington and his subsequent withdrawal to Winchester. Early on the morning of October 14, however, Mosby and his men stopped a train near Duffield Station in West Virginia and captured two Federal paymasters carrying $168,000 in cash. At the conclusion of the raid, they gathered at Ebenezer Church near Bloomfield to divide the profits among the men, with each receiving a $2,000 share. Lieutenant Charles Grogan later reported that the greenbacks "circulated so freely in Loudoun that

Ebenezer Church, where Mosby's men divided up the spoils of the Greenback Raid. *Photo by the author.*

never afterwards was there a pie or blooded horse sold in that section for Confederate money."[77] Because Mosby would not accept a share of the money for himself, the men pooled a portion of their funds, went to the Carter family's Oatlands Plantation just south of Leesburg, bought a horse Mosby had admired there and presented her to him.

There would be more skirmishes in Loudoun County in the last six months of the war, more men would die and more widows would grieve, but the county had seen its last full-fledged battle.

"The Terror of the Union People"

JOHN W. MOBBERLY OF LOUDOUN COUNTY

The roster of the Thirty-fifth Virginia Cavalry compiled by John Divine says that John Mobberly "deserted 9/1/64" and was "assassinated 4/5/65."[78] According to his tombstone, he was not yet twenty-one years old when he died. He was said to be a native of Loudoun County, but contemporary evidence of his life and death is restricted largely to his grave, a claim he made on the Confederate government for the cost of a horse that had been killed in the Battle of Brandy Station and a few cryptic notations on his battalion's roster.

Most of what we know about John Mobberly was written after the war, with very little based on firsthand knowledge. It is largely hearsay and exaggeration. There is much in his story to bring to mind the dime novel legends of Frank and Jesse James, the Younger brothers and Billy the Kid. One contemporary account said of him,

> This fellow Mobley [sic], whose acts of lawlessness have struck terror throughout the whole of Loudon [sic] and several other counties, is a smooth-faced, leaden-eyed, soulless man of unknown parentage; he was raised by a negro in Loudon, and almost his first act with which he commenced his career of crime was robbing his benefactor of two horses—the only means he had of obtaining a living.[79]

On a more positive note, Magnus Thompson, who rode with Mobberly in the Thirty-fifth Virginia Cavalry, said of him,

> He was brave, and I have often thought no sane man would have risked his life as Mobberly did. Of course, in battle, we took those chances willingly, but in his independent method he could use his own pleasure regarding an attack or retreat. But he attacked first, and if too big a job for him he would give them the road, and the devil could not catch him, as he was always superbly mounted.[80]

The most often-told Mobberly story is used to demonstrate his cruelty and total disregard for the rules of "civilized" warfare. According to this account, the men of the Loudoun Rangers were scattered around Waterford looking for something to eat when they were attacked by at least a hundred of Mosby's men. They had two men killed, five captured and a sergeant, Charles Stewart, severely wounded before the Southerners, in keeping with their hit-and-run tactics, withdrew with their prisoners.

As Mosby's men rode off to the south, Mobberly and his small "band of cutthroats" approached the town from their Short Hill Mountain sanctuary. When he came upon Sergeant Stewart lying wounded and helpless in the road, Mobberly began to ride his horse back and forth over him, gleefully firing at the prostrate form with a revolver. When he either ran out of ammunition or tired of the sport, Mobberly dismounted, relieved the sergeant of his new boots and rode away laughing loudly.

Miraculously, Stewart was still alive. He was carried to the nearby home of Miss Rachel Steele, where Dr. Thomas Bond treated him. Upon seeing the wounded man, the doctor cried out, "My only ambition in life is to live long enough to make another hell for the man that shot Stewart after he was helpless!"[81]

At another time a Unionist named Law disappeared from his home in Harpers Ferry, never to be seen again. Years after the war, an anonymous local resident "confessed" that he and other members of Mobberly's gang had taken Law to Short Hill Mountain and staked him out in the open to die of exposure or be eaten by wild beasts. Other accounts written soon after the war said that Mobberly rarely took prisoners, and those he did capture were likewise staked out to die on the mountain. Loudoun Ranger John W. Forsythe recorded in his 1892 memoirs that "a number of skeletons" were found in such a condition at the end of the war.[82]

These stories contrast sharply with other accounts of Mobberly as a Robin Hood figure, who fed and protected Southern sympathizers living under the heel of their Northern oppressors. It is also at variance with the image of Mobberly as a brave scout who more than once led White's Comanches on successful forays against the enemy and who, when his horse was killed at Brandy Station, leaped into the saddle behind a Union cavalryman, shot him dead and rode off on his enemy's horse.

No doubt Mobberly was neither as evil as Union accounts claim, nor as saintly as he is depicted in some Southern accounts. He was a child in a man's body, freed by the war from the restraints of civilization and exercising the power of life and death with a Colt revolver in his hand and a loyal band of henchmen at his side. Magnus Thompson boasted that Mobberly

> *killed more Yankees than any man in the Army of Northern Virginia. He damaged the enemy in loss of property, troops, etc., more than any one of record…that is to say, the damage he inflicted on them was one hundred thousand dollars a year.*

If this figure is even remotely accurate, it is no wonder Federal authorities were almost desperate to rid the county of Mobberly and his band. A number of ambushes were laid for him prior to the spring of 1865, but he escaped all of them. Thompson said he was always superbly mounted. Apparently, he was also incredibly lucky.

Briscoe Goodheart relates one such incident in which he says a squad of Rangers, learning where Mobberly would be the next day, "concealed themselves and waited [in ambush]." Mobberly soon appeared "with drawn saber, chasing a negro boy who was driving a cart. The boy was badly frightened, which Moberly [*sic*] seemed to enjoy." When the frightened boy and the guerrilla came abreast of their hiding place, the Rangers leaped to their feet and demanded Mobberly's surrender. Instead of complying with the demand, he "lay down in his saddle, put spurs to his swift-footed horse, and making a sharp turn in the road, darted out of sight." Goodheart admits that every Union man fired at the Rebel at close range "but did not strike him."

Another time, Mobberly was being pursued through "leg-deep drifts" of snow in a sleigh. To make his escape, he cut the traces and mounted one of the horses that was pulling the sleigh, once again escaping untouched by the volley of bullets fired in his direction.[83]

Finally, their inability to capture or kill Mobberly and his small band prompted Federal authorities to speak openly of offering a reward for his dead body. General John D. Stevenson, who was commanding the garrison at Harpers Ferry, wrote to the army chief of staff,

> *Some citizens of Loudoun have proposed to me that if I will arm them and give them the means of living away from home for awhile they will kill or capture the band…I think promising these men a reward of $1,000 for Mobberly and $500 for each of the others, dead or alive, will clean out the concern.*

The reply Stevenson received from Washington said, in part, that it was

> *not proper to offer a reward openly, but* [we] *will reward the men liberally in proportion to the service they may render…The general desires that the whole matter shall be kept secret.*[84]

Goodheart says that three civilians, including former Loudoun Ranger Jacob Boyrer, accepted the challenge to bring in Mobberly. Stevenson gave orders that they be accompanied by three active duty members of the Rangers, one of whom was the same Sergeant Charles Stewart, who Mobberly had so brutally assaulted the year before. Another of the civilians was Luther H. Potterfield, on whose farm the ambush would be laid. On the afternoon of April 5, 1865, Mobberly and Jim Riley, one of his men, rode into Potterfield's barnyard at the foot of Short Hill Mountain. As he approached, Stewart and five other men stepped out of the barn with revolvers drawn and cocked. Seeing them, Mobberly threw up his hands and said, "Oh, Lord, I am gone," as all six fired at him. He died instantly with three bullets in his head.

Because he had stopped outside the barnyard to water his horse, Riley was able to escape, wounded but alive. Stewart and his men threw Mobberly's body over his horse and delivered it to General Stevenson in Harpers Ferry. Stevenson put it on display outside his headquarters, where souvenir hunters cut away bits of the dead man's clothing until almost nothing remained.

According to Goodheart, the three civilians involved in the ambush received $1,000 plus expenses, while the three soldiers got nothing. Although the men were in Harpers

Ferry, safely beyond the reach of Mobberly's friends, Potterfield's barn was burned to the ground the next day.[85]

Eventually, Mobberly's body was released to his mother. Local tradition says that there was a grand funeral procession from the Mobberly Farm to Hillsboro, and from there out the Harpers Ferry Road to Salem Church. Sometime after the war, a headstone was placed over the grave, allegedly purchased by Henry Heaton, a former Mosby Ranger and postwar member of the Virginia General Assembly. Engraved on the stone are fifteen lines of florid praise:

> *God bless thee, brave soldier,*
> *Thy life's dream is o'er,*
> *Thou wilt do battle no more.*
> *To the land of the blessed*
> *Thou hast gone to depart,*
> *With a smile on thy face*
> *And a joy in thy heart.*
> *Thrice hallowed the green spot*
> *Where our hero is laid,*
> *His deeds from our memory*
> *Shall nevermore fade.*
> *The stranger will say,*
> *As he lingers around,*
> *'Tis the grave of a hero,*
> *'Tis liberty's mound.*

"There Is a God in Israel"

Throughout the war, the Quaker and German communities of northern Loudoun County remained staunchly loyal to the Union, greeting every Northern incursion into the county as liberation. Because the area around Lovettsville and Waterford was so close to the border between the North and South, neither side could maintain a permanent military presence there. Instead, raiding parties from both armies frequently visited the area to seize forage and provisions. Sometimes they paid for what they took; more often than not, they just loaded it into their wagons and drove away, leaving the hungry civilians to make do with what was left. Mosby's men, in particular, feeling no qualms about "taxing" the people they deemed disloyal, made frequent visits to the area between raids on General Phil Sheridan's army in the Shenandoah Valley in the fall of 1864.

As early as August 1864, General Ulysses Grant, the commander of all the Union armies, suggested to Sheridan,

> If you can possibly spare a division of cavalry, send them through Loudoun County, to destroy and carry off the crops, animals, negroes, and all men under fifty years of age capable of bearing arms.[86]

Sheridan, however, had his hands full dealing with Jubal Early and his army in Winchester. It was not until November, after Early had been defeated at Cedar Creek and Fisher's Hill, that Sheridan felt secure enough in the Shenandoah to turn his attention to Loudoun County. On November 26, he notified Washington, "I will soon commence work on Mosby…[in] Loudoun County, and let them know there is a God in Israel." On November 27, he ordered Major General Wesley Merritt to take a division of cavalry into Loudoun County and move along the base of the mountains from Upperville to the Potomac. Merritt was instructed to

> consume and destroy all forage and subsistence, burn all barns and mills and their contents, and drive off all stock in the region…This order must be literally executed,

bearing in mind, however, that no dwellings are to be burned and that no personal violence be offered to the citizens.[87]

Sheridan gave Merritt and his men four days to accomplish their mission.

Merritt's men entered the county in three groups, one passing through Ashby's Gap and moving south into Fauquier County toward Rectortown and Salem (now Marshall) before swinging back up toward Middleburg; another moving east on the Ashby's Gap Turnpike (Route 50) to Aldie and then up toward Snickersville; and the third entering through Snicker's Gap and heading north to the Potomac. Ironically, by remaining west of the Bull Run Mountains, they visited the worst destruction on the section of the county that was most loyal to the Union: the Quaker and German settlements. They did their work well, setting fire to barns, corncribs and hayricks and herding off cattle, horses and sheep taken from all the citizens, whether loyal or not. They butchered or, in some cases, burned alive all the pigs and poultry they could not herd like the other livestock.

According to Ranger James Williamson,

From Monday afternoon, November 28th, until Friday morning, December 2d, they ranged through the beautiful Valley of Loudoun and a portion of Fauquier County, burning and laying waste. They robbed the people of everything they could destroy or carry off—horses, cows, cattle, sheep, hogs, etc...They burned all the mills and factories, as well as hay, wheat, corn, straw and every description of forage. Barns and stables, whether full or empty, were burned.[88]

Nearly all the mills in the county were consumed by the flames. One, however, was saved by Brigadier General Thomas Devin. David Mansfield was a Quaker who had provided food and shelter to Devin and his staff on an earlier visit to the area. The general knocked on his door and warned Mansfield to fill as many buckets as he could find with water in case the flames from his mill should spread to his house. Devin then had his adjutant pile dry wood against the outer wall of the mill and set it on fire. As it began to burn, the two Union officers quickly rode away. Mansfield used the water to douse the flames before much damage was done. In the words of the adjutant, "Thus Gen. Devin was made happy, and a loyal man fully repaid for his generous hospitality."[89]

Overall, the people of Waterford and Lovettsville were astonished that such loss and destruction of property should be their lot in view of their loyalty to the national government. Some, however, realized that the food grown by a Union man was just as nourishing to Mosby's partisans as the food of a secessionist, and if the Rebels were to be driven from the area, both would have to be denied them. Major J.B. Wheeler of the Sixth New York Cavalry recalled that,

At Waterford...two young ladies perched on the wide gate posts in front of their home, waving American flags and said as their hay was being destroyed, "Burn away, burn away, if it will keep Mosby from coming here!"[90]

Sally's Mill near Middleburg. These are the ruins of one of Loudoun's mills destroyed during the burning raid. *Photo by the author.*

It did not, of course, keep Mosby from operating in the area. In that one week, Loudoun County suffered more destruction and loss of property than it had seen in the previous three years, but the guerrillas continued to operate as before. They hovered around the flanks of Merritt's burning parties, doing what little damage they could in quick hit-and-run attacks, and they helped the civilians save what they could of their stock. Williamson said,

In many instances, after the first day of the burning, we would run off stock from the path of the raiders into the limits of the district already burned over, and there it was kept undisturbed or in a situation where it could be more easily driven off and concealed. We also annoyed the raiders considerably by hovering around them in small squads and suddenly dashing in among them, whenever an opportunity offered, shooting on all sides and then scampering off.[91]

By the time Merritt's men left Loudoun County, the destruction was extensive in the limited area they visited. Although Merritt did not provide detailed figures, his report to Sheridan indicated:

From 5,000 to 6,000 head of cattle, including from 3,000 to 4,000 head of sheep and nearly 1,000 head of fatted hogs…were driven off or destroyed. From 500 to 700 horses, including mares and colts, were also brought away.[92]

Only the reserve brigade provided a detailed report of their operations for the week. They claimed to have destroyed 230 barns, 8 mills, a distillery, 10,000 tons of hay and 25,000 bushels of grain, in addition to taking 87 horses, 474 cattle and 100 sheep. The total cost to the people of Loudoun was estimated at $411,620.[93] Samuel Janney estimated that the loss to

Union men was, for property burned $196,000, and for live stock taken away, about $60,000. That sustained by Friends of our Monthly Meeting at Goose Creek, was about $80,000, and by members of the Fairfax Monthly Meeting (held at Waterford), $23,000.[94]

It would take nearly eight years for Loudoun Friends to receive restitution from the government in the amount of roughly $62,000 to pay for their lost stock. They were never paid for the property the raiders destroyed.

Despite the devastation, the people of Loudoun remained remarkably optimistic. The *Waterford News*, an underground newspaper published by three young Quaker women, said,

We do not believe, if our Government had been as well acquainted with us as we are with ourselves, the order for the recent burning would have been issued; but having suffered so much at the hands of the Rebels ever since the commencement of this cruel war, we will cheerfully submit to what we feel assured our Government thought was a military necessity.[95]

"There Is a God in Israel"

On the other side of the loyalty coin, Ida Dulany said,

> *In spite of it all I could but remark the cheerfulness with which the devastation was borne by all the inhabitants. I did not see one sad face. At night in looking at what my neighbors, many of whom were poor, many widows, many soldiers' families, were suffering, I felt like crying out to God for a just judgment on the wicked minds that contrived and the ruthless hands that wrought such a work. As to our own loss I was only grateful it was no greater.*

The Long Road to Recovery

Less than a month after the burning raid, Brigadier General Thomas Devin moved his brigade to the vicinity of Lovettsville for the winter. In the raid's aftermath, he was forced to haul food and forage for his men and horses across the Potomac from Maryland. Devin was welcomed by the loyal residents of the county, but even the secessionists suffered little from his presence. Frank Myers said of him:

> *About Christmas a Federal brigade, commanded by General Deven* [sic], *had established itself in winter quarters near Lovettsville…, and during the time they were there these troops had treated the inhabitants of the country through which they scouted and foraged with far more courtesy and consideration than was the custom of Federal soldiers south of the Potomac…but as a general thing Deven showed that his warfare was not upon helpless citizens, whose persons and property were entirely at his mercy, and in this respect proved himself an exception to the majority of commanding officers in the abolition crusade upon the South, who only limited their license to the extent of their power.*[96]

Devin continued to treat the citizens well despite the fact that his picket posts were raided almost nightly by John Mobberly and his gang. On the night of February 17, 1865, Elijah White led an attack on the camp of the Sixth New York Cavalry that almost ended in disaster for him when the post he thought was manned by only a hundred or so men turned out to have been reinforced by several hundred more. This was the Thirty-fifth Virginia Cavalry's last action in Loudoun County, and their last as an independent command. They soon returned to the Army of Northern Virginia and remained there until Lee's surrender at Appomattox in April. Mosby and his men fought only once more in the county, attacking a mixed command of infantry and cavalry near Harmony (now Hamilton) on March 22 and 23. After that, aside from minor skirmishes, the fighting was over in Loudoun County.

PEACE AT LAST

On April 12, word arrived that General Lee had surrendered his army to Grant and Meade at Appomattox Court House. A group of men who were gathered in a shoe shop on Waterford's Main Street, upon hearing the news, ran out into the street, laughing and cheering, and "grabbing each other by the arms, these black-frocked sedate Quakers, momentarily forgetting the tenets of their Meeting, danced a jig."[97] On May 7, with the town decorated with patriotic bunting and a picnic lunch spread out for everyone, the residents of Waterford celebrated a formal raising of the U.S. flag "as an emblem of Peace & safety," according to the diary of Rebecca Williams. She continued, "Stores are open and it seems like the good times before the war."

In June 1865 the Quaker community known as Goose Creek finally got the post office for which it had originally petitioned in 1861. With the new post office, the name of the village was changed to Lincoln; the first of many towns across the country to be named for the martyred president.

Not everyone in the county was as pleased with the war's outcome as the people of the Quaker and German communities. There were no celebrations and dances for the secessionists who had been in the majority in 1861. With their farms devastated, their slaves freed and their livestock run off or killed, local secessionists were financially ruined. Those who had been wealthy before the war were as poor as all the rest because most of them had patriotically invested their money in Confederate bonds, which were rendered completely worthless by the defeat. Large landowners found themselves temporarily without laborers to rebuild their barns and mills and put in a new crop. John Townsend Trowbridge, a Bostonian who traveled extensively throughout the South after the war, could have been describing the Loudoun Valley in 1866 when he wrote of the Shenandoah,

The wealthiest people are now the poorest. With hundreds of acres they can't raise a dollar. Their slaves have left them, and they have no money, even if they have the disposition, to hire the freed people.[98]

The return of paroled veterans from Lee's army did little to ease the situation. The soldiers had farms of their own to restore and families to feed and clothe. Accustomed to fending for themselves, they were not likely to take a job as a laborer for another man. The terms given to Lee by General Grant specified that officers and cavalrymen were allowed to take their horses home with them, but the infantrymen made the long walk from Appomattox to Loudoun with little more than the clothes on their backs. They arrived to find that they had no way to haul firewood or plow their fields, other than a few oxen shared between farms for such essential tasks. Still, they came home determined to do whatever it took to get back on their feet. Times would be hard in the county for several years, but Loudoun would eventually recover thanks to the dogged determination of her citizens.

THE CONFISCATION SCARE

Only four months after Lee surrendered at Appomattox, Major General Oliver O. Howard issued a proclamation in his capacity as commissioner of the new Bureau of Refugees, Freedmen and Abandoned Lands (better known as the Freedman's Bureau). The *Democratic Mirror* reported,

> *We find in the Richmond Republic of Friday last, over five columns of advertised property confiscated in Virginia by the United States Government, two and a half* [columns] *of which, embracing 81 pieces, are in Loudoun County alone.*[99]

Among the men whose property was to be confiscated and given to former slaves were John W. Fairfax, whose Oak Hill home was the former residence of President James Monroe; Charles Berkley, a former officer of the Eighth Virginia Infantry; Francis Mason, the grandson of George Mason and an author of the Bill of Rights; and George W. Ball, the nephew of George Washington. The newspaper's editor noted that the men were reluctant to begin repairing the ravages of war on their homes and farms as long as they were in danger of losing them at any minute. President Johnson opposed the wholesale confiscation of property, however, and many in Congress questioned the constitutionality of taking land from a man who had not been convicted of a crime. In the end, none of the land belonging to Loudoun County farmers and planters was taken.

EMANCIPATION

Because of its location on the border between the Union and the Confederacy, news of Abraham Lincoln's Emancipation Proclamation had come early to Loudoun County's black population. Some left their old homes during the war and went north, either to find work or to volunteer to serve in the Union armies. Poor record keeping makes it impossible to state with certainty how many former Loudoun County slaves fought for the freedom of their race, but veterans of several U.S. Colored Troops regiments now lie in local cemeteries.

The most important institutions in the lives of the newly freed people of color were home, church and community, with the latter often being organized around the schools they had been forbidden to attend in their years in bondage. The first of five freedmen's schools was established in Waterford by Sarah Steer in 1865 and listed nearly as many adults as children among its students.[100] In the years following the war, African Americans who had been relegated to the balconies of predominantly white churches in the past started their own congregations, with thirty-one such churches established between 1865 and 1900—an indication of their growing self-reliance.

While there was a distinct social separation of the black and white races, there was little physical segregation. The census records and tax rolls of the postwar period show blacks, whites and mulattoes mingled together throughout the county. Still, some predominantly black communities sprang up as the former slaves began to settle on their own land, which was often sold or given to them by their former owners. Many of the freedmen worked for wages for large landowners or hired themselves out performing trades they had learned in bondage. The majority of the county's blacksmiths, stonemasons, gardeners, carpenters, cooks and seamstresses in the latter quarter of the nineteenth century were African American. By 1900, however, a large number of African Americans were farmers, 67 percent of whom owned their own land.

RECONSTRUCTION

On March 2, 1867, the U.S. Congress, still seeking revenge for the assassination of Abraham Lincoln, passed the Reconstruction Act under which Virginia became Military District Number One, under the command of Major General John M. Schofield. Although the law disenfranchised senior Confederate officers and required other former soldiers to swear a loyalty oath to the U.S. government before they could hold public office or register to vote, Virginia was fortunate to have Schofield in charge. Richard Lee Morton wrote of him:

> *He was conservative, just and wise; and it was due to his moral courage that Virginia was spared the reign of terror that existed in most Southern States during the Reconstruction period. His policy was to gain the confidence and support of the people of the State and to interfere as little as possible with civil authorities.*[101]

Reconstruction ended in Virginia in January 1876 when the state became the eighth former Confederate state officially returned to the Union. Though this might be considered the actual end of the Civil War, the ensuing unfortunate era of Jim Crow laws and legally mandated segregation would continue well into the twentieth century.

REST IN PEACE

The last surviving Confederate veteran in Loudoun County, Dr. James E. Copeland of Round Hill, died January 16, 1937, at the age of ninety-one, but neither he, nor the men who served with him, have been forgotten. Like most Virginia counties, Loudoun has its monuments to her sons who served in the armies of the Confederacy. The first was erected in 1866 to honor the unknown soldiers buried in the Sharon Cemetery in Middleburg, many of whom had died in that town of wounds received at Second Manassas. The second was put up by the State of Mississippi in the Union Cemetery in Leesburg in 1877 as a memorial to the men of that state who died at Ball's Bluff, "and to the many noble sons of Loudoun who fell and were left on the field of battle."

In 1884, a similar monument was erected in the Ivy Hill Cemetery in Upperville, the site of some of the hardest fighting in the June 1863 Loudoun Valley Campaign. The county's only monument to Union dead was placed on the Aldie battlefield by the First

Major General John Schofield, commander of Military District Number One under the 1867 Reconstruction Act. *Courtesy of the USAMHI.*

Confederate Circle and monument to the Unknown Dead in Middleburg's Sharon Cemetery. *Photo by the author.*

Massachusetts Cavalry Association in June 1891 on a piece of ground given to them by Dallas Furr, a former member of Mosby's Rangers. In 1908, as the generation of veterans began to die off in increasing numbers, the county placed a monument to its Confederate soldiers on the courthouse lawn in Leesburg. Sometime later, two markers were placed on the Ball's Bluff Battlefield: one to mark the site of Colonel Edward Baker's death, and the other in honor of Clinton Hatcher, the color-bearer of the Eighth Virginia Infantry, who was also killed in the fighting.

Another Civil War monument was placed in front of the National Sporting Library in Middleburg in 1999 to honor the 1.5 million horses and mules that were killed during the war. A smaller version of the monument that was erected in front of the Virginia Historical Society in Richmond, the statue was a gift of the Mellon Foundation. The Eighth Virginia Infantry Memorial at Ball's Bluff joined the First Massachusetts marker as one of Loudoun County's only two battlefield monuments in September 2007.

The most lasting tribute to the men and women who endured or died in four years of warfare in Loudoun County is the land itself. North and South alike hallowed the land with their blood and watered it with their tears. We who follow owe it to them not to let their memory fade or the sacred sites of their struggle be destroyed.

The Mississippi monument in Leesburg's Union Cemetery. *Photo by the author.*

Confederate graves and monument in Upperville's Ivy Hill Cemetery. *Photo by the author.*

The First Massachusetts Cavalry monument on the Aldie Battlefield. It is one of only two battlefield monuments in Loudoun County. The monument was erected in 1891 on ground donated by Dallas Furr, a veteran of Mosby's Rangers. *Photo by the author.*

A Confederate monument on the Old Courthouse lawn in Leesburg. *Photo by the author.*

The Edward Baker marker on the Ball's Bluff Battlefield. The marker incorrectly identifies the spot where Colonel Baker was killed. *Photo by the author.*

The Clinton Hatcher marker on the Ball's Bluff Battlefield. No one knows precisely where or when in the fighting Hatcher was killed. *Photo by the author.*

A monument erected in Middleburg by Paul Mellon in memory of the 1.5 million horses and mules that died during the American Civil War. *Photo by the author.*

The Eighth Virginia Infantry monument placed on the Ball's Bluff Battlefield in September 2007. *Photo by the author.*

Notes

Introduction

1. Walker Percy, "The American War," *Commonweal* 65 (March 29, 1957): 655–57; Republished in Patrick Samway, ed., *Signposts in a Strange Land* (New York: Picador, 1991).
2. Rebecca Williams, *Papers of Mary Francis Dutton Steer (1840–1933) of Waterford, Virginia*, Courtesy of the Waterford Foundation, 53.

The English Come to Loudoun

3. Fairfax Harrison, *The Proprietors of the Northern Neck: Chapters of Culpeper Genealogy* (Richmond, VA: Old Dominion Press, 1926).
4. James W. Head, *History and Comprehensive Description of Loudoun County Virginia* (Baltimore, MD: Genealogical Publishing Co., 1908), 113.

Slavery and Abolition in Loudoun County

5. Compiled from the 1850 county tax rolls and U.S. Census Slave Schedule.
6. Thomas Earl, *Life, Travels and Opinions of Benjamin Lundy* (Philadelphia: William D. Parrish, 1847), 218.
7. Stephen B. Weeks, "Anti-slavery Sentiment in the South," in *Publication of the Southern History Association* II, 2 (April 1898).
8. Yardley Taylor file, Thomas Balch Library, Leesburg, VA.
9. *George Carter Letterbook*, p. 201, Virginia Historical Society, Richmond, VA. Transcript at Oatlands Plantation, Leesburg, VA.
10. *The Democratic Mirror* (Leesburg, VA), December 7, 1859.

Politics and Secession

11. *The Democratic Mirror*, January 25, 1860.
12. *Proceedings of the Virginia State Convention of 1861*, Library of Virginia, Richmond.
13. *The Democratic Mirror*, May 29, 1861.
14. Williams, *Papers of Mary Steer*.

Loudoun Prepares for War

15. *The Democratic Mirror*, May 15, 1861.
16. Southern Historical Society Papers, January–December 1886, Vol. XIV, Richmond, VA, 217.
17. *The Democratic Mirror*, April 17, 1861.
18. Ibid., April 24, 1861.
19. Head, *History*, 149.

The Dogs of War Let Loose

20. Robert N. Scott; H.M. Lazelle; George B. Davis; Leslie J. Perry; Joseph W. Kirkley; Fred C. Ainsworth; John S. Moodey; Calvin D. Cowles; United States War Dept.; United States War Records Office; United States Record and Pension Office; United States Congress House. The War of the Rebellion: A Compilation of the Official Records of the Union and Confederate Armies, Series 1, Vol. II, Chapter IX, (Washington, DC: Government Print Office, 1880–1901), 872. (Hereafter cited as Official Records.)
21. *Autobiography of Eppa Hunton* (Richmond, VA: William Byrd Press, 1933), 25–26.
22. *The Democratic Mirror*, June 12, 1861.
23. *Hunton Autobiography*, 28.
24. The Journal of Ida Powell Dulany, Unpublished.
25. *Hunton Autobiography*, p. 27.

Ball's Bluff: "A Very Nice Little Military Chance"

26. McClellan to Stone, "The Battle of Ball's Bluff," *Report of the Joint Committee on the Conduct of the War* (Milwood, NY: Kraus Reprint Co., 1977), 252–53. (Hereafter referred to as *JCCW*.)
27. *Official Records*, Series 1, Volume V, 347.
28. Testimony of Colonel Charles Devens, *JCCW*, 403.
29. Testimony of Lieutenant Church Howe, *JCCW*, 375.
30. Testimony of Brigadier General Charles P. Stone, *JCCW*, 277.
31. *Official Records*, Series 1, Vol. V, 294.
32. Devens testimony, *JCCW*, 405.

33. Howe testimony, *JCCW*, 376.

34. Elijah White speech, Miscellany Collection, Thomas Balch Library, Leesburg, VA.

GATEWAY TO WAR

35. All quotes in this account taken from *Official Records*, Series 1, Vol. V.

36. *Official Records*, Series 1, Vol. V, 733.

37. Williams, *Papers of Mary Steer*, 200.

38. *Loudoun County Minute Book* 16, 72.

39. Williams, *Papers of Mary Steer*, 224.

40. *Official Records*, Series 1, Vol. V, 549.

41. Joseph G. Bilby, "Load the Hopper and Turn the Crank," *America's Civil War* 20, 3 (July 2007).

42. *Official Records*, Series 1, Vol. V, 549.

TWO MEN ON OPPOSITE SIDES

43. William N. McDonald, *A History of the Laurel Brigade* (Frederick, MD: Olde Soldier Books, Reprinted 1987), 29.

44. Briscoe Goodheart, *History of the Independent Loudoun Rangers* (Washington, DC: McGill & Wallace, 1896), 27.

45. Ibid., 123.

46. Frank M. Myers, *The Comanches* (Baltimore, MD: Kelly, Piet & Co., 1871), 98–102.

47. Head, *History*, 153.

TO ANTIETAM: THE MARYLAND CAMPAIGN OF 1862

48. *Official Records*, Series 1, Volume XVI, 749.

49. *Official Records*, Series 1, Vol. XIX/2, 590.

50. Major Albert J. Myer, Chief Signal Officer, U.S. Army, reported that "Lieutenant Miner occup[ying] the summit of Sugar Loaf…reported…their crossing the Potomac near the Monocacy, and the commencement of their movement into Maryland." See *Official Records*, Series 1, Vol. XIX/1, 118.

51. George M. Neese, *Three Years in the Confederate Horse Artillery* (Washington: Neale Publishing Co., 1911), 111.

52. *Official Records*, Series 1, Vol. XIX/1, 1092.

53. Myers, *The Comanches*, 111; *Official Records*, Series 1, Vol. XIX/1, 1092.

54. Henry Kyd Douglas, *I Rode with Stonewall* (Marietta, GA: Mockingbird Books, 1995), 188.

55. *Official Records*, Series 1, Vol. XIX/2, 142.

56. Margaret Ann Vogtsberger, *The Dulanys of Welbourne* (Berryville, VA: Rockbridge Publishing Co., 1995), 55.

INTRODUCING MOSBY'S RANGERS: THE WINTER OF 1862–63

57. John W. Munson, *Reminiscences of a Mosby Guerrilla* (New York: Moffat, Yard & Co., 1906), 42.
58. Josiah Grout, *Memoir of General William Wallace Grout and Autobiography of Josiah Grout* (Newport, VT: Bullock Press, 1919).
59. John S. Mosby, *The Memoirs of Colonel John S. Mosby* (Gaithersburg, MD: Olde Soldier Books, Reprint 1987).
60. Munson, *Reminiscences*, 56.

PRELUDE TO GETTYSBURG

61. *Official Records*, Series 1, Vol. XXVII/3, 172.
62. Letter, June 23, 1863, The Alfred Pleasonton Papers, Library of Congress.
63. *Philadelphia Weekly Times*, February 8, 1879.
64. John S. Mosby, *Stuart's Cavalry in the Gettysburg Campaign* (New York: Moffat, Yard and Co., 1908).
65. *Official Records*, Series 1, Vol. XXVII/2, 690.
66. *Philadelphia Weekly Times*, February 21, 1880.
67. *Official Records*, Series 1, Vol. XXVII/1, 201.

MOSBY'S CONFEDERACY

68. James J. Williamson, *Mosby's Rangers* (New York: Sturgis & Walton, 1909), 129.
69. Thomas H. Merry, letter to *Alta California*, San Francisco, published July 17, 1863.
70. Williamson, *Mosby's Rangers*, 142.
71. Munson, *Reminiscences*, 86.
72. John H. Alexander, *Mosby's Men* (New York: Neale Publishing, 1907), 88.
73. Munson, *Reminiscences*, 96.
74. Larry Rogers and Keith Rogers, eds., *Their Horses Climbed Trees* (Atglen, PA: Schiffer Military History, 2001), 281.
75. *Official Records*, Series 1, Vol. XXXVII/1, 359.
76. Williamson, *Mosby's Rangers*, 188.
77. Ibid., 263.

"THE TERROR OF THE UNION PEOPLE": JOHN W. MOBBERLY OF LOUDOUN COUNTY

78. John Divine, *35th Battalion, Virginia Cavalry* (Virginia Regimental History Series, H.E. Howard, 1985).

79. E.A. Paul, *New York Times*, February 9, 1865, quoted in Richard E. Crouch, *Rough Riding Scout* (Arlington, VA: Elden Editions, 1994), 4.

80. *Confederate Veteran*, Vol. XXVII, 288.

81. Goodheart, *History*, 127.

82. John W. Forsythe, *Guerrilla Warfare and Life in Libby Prison* (N.p., 1892). Despite Forsythe's claim, there are no verifiable accounts of human remains ever being found on Short Hill Mountain in such a condition.

83. Joseph Barry, *The Strange History of Harpers Ferry* (Shepherdstown, WV: Shepherdstown Register, 1903), 127.

84. *Official Records*, Series 1, Vol. XLVI/3, 445.

85. Goodheart, *History*, 196.

"There Is a God in Israel"

86. *Official Records*, Series I, Vol. XLIII/1, 811.

87. Ibid., 679.

88. Williamson, *Mosby's Rangers*, 319

89. Taylor M. Chamberlin, *Where Did They Stand?* (Waterford, VA: Waterford Foundation, 2003).

90. Emma H. Conrow, "Girls Published Civil War Newspaper," *Baltimore American*, February 5, 1922, C-3.

91. Williamson, *Mosby's Rangers*, 322.

92. *Official Records*, Series I, Vol. XLIII/1, 730.

93. Ibid., 673.

94. Samuel M. Janney, *Memoirs of Samuel M. Janney* (Philadelphia: Friends Book Association, 1881), 230.

95. *Waterford News*, January 28, 1865.

The Long Road to Recovery

96. Myers, *The Comanches*, 270.

97. George E. Bentley, *Waterford Perspectives* (Waterford, VA: Waterford Foundation, 1983).

98. John T. Trowbridge, *The South* (Macon, GA: Mercer University Press, 2006), 69.

99. *Loudoun Democratic Mirror*, August 31, 1865.

100. *Friends Intelligencer*, vol. XX, Waterford Foundation Archives, 250–251

101. Richard L. Morton, *The Negro in Virginia Politics, 1865–1902* (Charlottesville: University of Virginia Press, 1919), 27.

Bibliography

BOOKS AND ARTICLES

Alexander, John H. *Mosby's Men*. New York: Neale Publishing, 1907.

Autobiography of Eppa Hunton. Richmond, VA: William Byrd Press, 1933.

Barry, Joseph. *The Strange History of Harpers Ferry*. Shepherdstown, WV: Shepherdstown Register, 1903.

"Battle of Ball's Bluff." *Report of the Joint Committee on the Conduct of the War (JCCW)*. Milwood, NY: Kraus Reprint Co., 1977.

Bentley, George E. *Waterford Perspectives*. Waterford, VA: Waterford Foundation, 1983.

Chamberlin, Taylor M. *Where Did They Stand?* Waterford, VA: Waterford Foundation, 2003.

Divine, John. *35th Battalion, Virginia Cavalry*. Virginia Regimental History Series. H.E. Howard, 1985.

Douglas, Henry Kyd. *I Rode with Stonewall*. Marietta, GA: Mockingbird Books, 1995.

Earl, Thomas. *Life, Travels and Opinions of Benjamin Lundy*. Philadelphia: William D. Parrish, 1847.

Fairfax, Harrison. *The Proprietors of the Northern Neck: Chapters of Culpeper Genealogy*. Richmond, VA: Old Dominion Press, 1926.

Forsythe, John W. *Guerrilla Warfare and Life in Libby Prison*. N.p., 1892.

Goodheart, Briscoe. *History of the Independent Loudoun Rangers*. Washington, DC: McGill & Wallace, 1896.

Grout, Josiah. *Memoir of General William Wallace Grout and Autobiography of Josiah Grout*. Newport, VT: Bullock Press, 1919.

Head, James W. *History and Comprehensive Description of Loudoun County Virginia*. Baltimore, MD: Genealogical Publishing Co., 1908.

Janney, Samuel M. *Memoirs of Samuel M. Janney*. Philadelphia: Friends Book Association, 1881.

McDonald, William N. *A History of the Laurel Brigade*. Frederick, MD: Olde Soldier Books, Reprinted 1987.

Morgan, James A., III. *A Little Short of Boats: the Fights at Ball's Bluff and Edwards Ferry, October 21–22, 1861*. Columbus, OH: Ironclad Publishing Co., 2004.

Morton, Richard L. *The Negro in Virginia Politics, 1865–1902*. Charlottesville: University of Virginia Press, 1919.

Mosby, John S. *The Memoirs of Colonel John S. Mosby*. Gaithersburg, MD: Olde Soldier Books, Reprint 1987.

———. *Stuart's Cavalry in the Gettysburg Campaign*. New York: Moffat, Yard & Co., 1908.

Munson, John W. *Reminiscences of a Mosby Guerrilla*. New York: Moffat, Yard & Co., 1906.

Myers, Frank M. *The Comanches*. Baltimore, MD: Kelly, Piet & Co., 1871.

Neese, George M. *Three Years in the Confederate Horse Artillery*. Washington, DC: Neale Publishing Co., 1911.

Percy, Walker. "The American War." *Commonweal* 65 (March 29, 1957): 655–57; Republished in Patrick Samway, ed. *Signposts in a Strange Land*. New York: Farrar, Straus and Giroux, 1991.

Proceedings of the Virginia State Convention of 1861. Richmond: Library of Virginia, 1861.

Rogers, Larry, and Keith Rogers, eds. *Their Horses Climbed Trees*. Atglen, PA: Schiffer Military History, 2001.

Scott, Robert N.; H.M. Lazelle; George B. Davis; Leslie J. Perry; Joseph W. Kirkley; Fred C. Ainsworth; John S. Moodey; Calvin D. Cowles; United States War Dept.; United States War Records Office; United States Record and Pension Office; United States Congress House. The War of the Rebellion: A Compilation of the Official Records of the Union and Confederate Armies. Washington, DC: Government Print Office, 1880–1901.

Southern Historical Society Papers vol. XIV. Richmond, VA: Southern Historical Society, January–December 1886.

Trowbridge, John T. *The South*. Macon, GA: Mercer University Press, 2006.

Vogtsberger, Margaret Ann. *The Dulanys of Welbourne*. Berryville, VA: Rockbridge Publishing Co., 1995.

Weeks, Stephen B. "Anti-slavery Sentiment in the South." Southern History Association Publications 2, 103.

Williamson, James J. *Mosby's Rangers*. New York: Sturgis & Walton, 1909.

NEWSPAPERS AND PERIODICALS

Alta California
America's Civil War
Baltimore American, February 5, 1922.
Confederate Veteran
Friends Intelligencer
Loudoun County Minute Book
Loudoun Democratic Mirror
New York Times
Philadelphia Weekly Times
Waterford News

UNPUBLISHED

Alfred Pleasonton Papers. Library of Congress.

Elijah White speech. Miscellany Collection. Thomas Balch Library, Leesburg, VA.

George Carter Letterbook. Virginia Historical Society, Richmond, VA. Transcript at Oatlands Plantation, Leesburg, VA.

The Journal of Ida Powell Dulany. Courtesy of the Charles Mackall family.

Williams, Rebecca. *Papers of Mary Frances Dutton Steer (1840–1933) of Waterford, Virginia.* Courtesy of the Waterford Foundation.

Yardley Taylor file. Thomas Balch Library, Leesburg, VA.

Index